To Love a Gentle Giant

Stories compiled by
Millie Spillers

"The greatness of a nation and its moral progress
can be judged by the way its animals are treated."
Mahatma Ghandi (1869-1948)

ISBN: 1479229709
ISBN-13: 978-1479229703

Cover photo courtesy of Alexis Peel Photography.

DEDICATION

Proceeds from this book will benefit
Rescue Foundation Incorporated (RFI Rescue)…
a rescue program for English Mastiffs only,
based in Penfield, NY. (www.mcoarescue.com)

"Stay back Mom, there's a mad goat next door"

Sampson & his Pawfest winnings

Mom
I'm tellin ya,
Dogs
don't
shower !!

TABLE OF CONTENTS

31. Emma - Connie Halket - Holyoke, MA
32. Digby - Don Crumb - Penfield, NY
34. Stella - Don Crumb - Penfield, NY
35. Jacob - Don Crumb - Penfield, NY
36. Cleo - Don Crumb - Penfield, NY
37. Cloey - Don Crumb - Penfield, NY
38. Bear and Zyta - Don Crumb - Penfield, NY
39. Hattie - Don Crumb - Penfield, NY
40. Hestia - Dusty Kenly - Waco, KY
41. Monty and Chloe - Patti Miller - Phoenix, AZ
42. Georgia-Girl and Figgie-Fig - Tania Palmer - Summerville, SC
43. Laird Duncan - Madeline Walkos - Chagrin Falls, OH
44. Shambeau - John Preston Smith - Huntington, WV
45. Izzy - Miranda Miller - Indian Trail, NC
46. Henry Sue - Cheryl Winters-Heard - Mobile, AL
47. Annabelle - Linda Hartman
48. Harmony - Melinda Kemppainen - Lawrence, KS
49. Major - Terri Latva - Gunter, TX
50. Cromwell - John and Natasha Jenkins - Norfolk, England
51. Custard - Sue Epps - Queenborough, Kent, England
52. Tonka - Sherry Eisenhuth - Tampa, FL
53. Brad Pitt - Robson Trujillo Marconi - Brazil
54. Sheeba, Bronson & Saber - Laura and Gary Anderson - Beloit, OH
55. Mugsy - Terri Runt - Freeport, IL
56. Fannie - Tamara Berry - Montello, WI
57. Nala - Yvonne Jensen - Oroville, CA
58. Little Man - Dean Jensen - Oroville, CA
59. BBB - Christina Jones - Reynoldsburg, OH
60. Riley - Jay Cruz - Hauppauge, NY
61. Winston - Rebecca Deaver - Clanton, AL

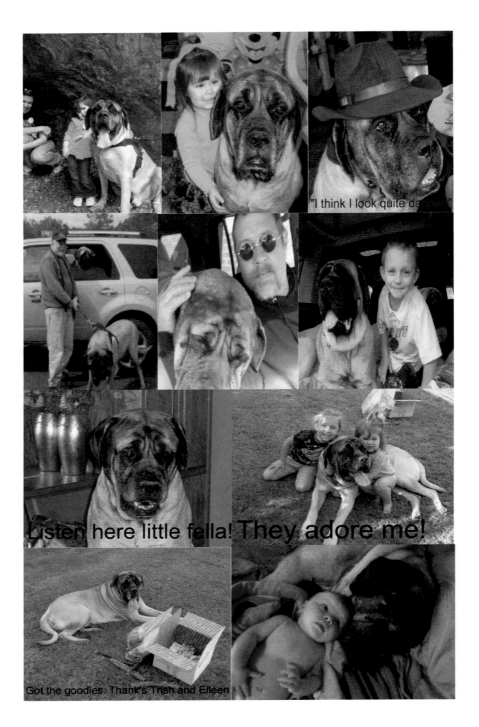

"I think I look quite dapper"

Listen here little fella! They adore me!

Got the goodies. Thank's Trish and Eileen

FOREWORD

Sampson

I have been an English Mastiff owner for 12 years and have found them to be God's most amazing, loving and loyal creatures.

Most Mastiff owners would agree that once you own a Mastiff, there's no going back, for no other breed can compare.

Personally I cannot imagine my life without a Mastiff in it.

Currently I have Sampson, a large fawn male that I rescued in September of 2010. At the time, I didn't realize that he would become my saving grace.

I lost my sweet 22-month-old Dante in April 2011 and could not have survived the pain without the love of Sampson.

I have many people to thank for giving me this wonderful boy. Here's his story:

Sampson lived with a business man who never showed him any love or attention. He was kept in a backyard for four years with no doghouse or any refuge from the cold, rain, heat or storms. Sometimes the man would leave on business trips for days at a time and forget to have someone come over to feed or water Sampson.

One day the man had to move and had no plans on taking Sampson with him. He told a young lady who worked for him to take Sampson to the pound. Fortunately she had a heart, and took Sampson to her mother's house instead. They loved and cared for him, but unfortunately one year later due to life circumstances, they had to let him go. These beautiful people reached out for help in finding him a loving and forever home, and this is how I learned of him.

One night while checking up on Facebook, I saw a beautiful, yet lonely face. His name was Sampson, and I knew he had to be mine. I already owned a one-year-old Mastiff named Dante that I loved dearly, but I was tiring of his constant need to play. This could be the answer. Luckily, the person that posted him was a friend, and I immediately typed that I wanted him. We shared this with our mutual friends on Facebook and everyone was happy for Sampson and me. But there was one big problem; Sampson was in Amarillo, Texas, and I live in Dacula, Georgia. I did not want to put Sampson through the stress of being shipped, and I could not get off work for the time it would take to drive and pick him up.

When my Facebook friends learned of my plight, they started volunteering to drive him to me. The rescuer in Texas planned and coordinated the two-day trip with eight volunteers. I was so touched that people I only knew on a computer screen were willing to do so much. Unfortunately on the first day of transport, there was an accident. The rescuer and his mother made a pitstop behind a gas station for Sampson to do his business. The mother was holding the leash and had it wrapped around her hand, when a semi truck came around the corner startling Sampson, and he bolted. The leash constricted with a mighty force and broke her hand. On the way to the emergency room, they called the next volunteer to let her know they would not be able to meet her as scheduled and would have to notify all other volunteers to reschedule. This amazing volunteer did not want anything to disrupt getting Sampson to me, and she volunteered to drive the extra hours to pick him up.

Pictures were taken at each hand-off and posted on Facebook. Hundreds of people all around the world were following this story and cheering for Sampson to make it to Georgia. The last volunteer drove an amazing eight hours and met me just one mile from my house. My husband and one-year-old Mastiff, Dante, went with me to pick him up. We parked at a Walmart beside a large open field, and the transporter parked a few spaces down. My husband took Dante for a walk in the field so I could meet Sampson one on one. When the back door opened and Sampson slowly emerged, I could not hold back my tears. He was everything I hoped he would be. I looked into those beautiful eyes, the same ones that spoke to me on a computer screen, and I said, "Hey Sampson, you are finally home!" I will forever be grateful to all the beautiful people who helped bring Sampson to me and for renewing my faith in mankind. I tried to send people money for their gas and time, but no one would accept the offer. In honor of them, I hope this book will pay it forward to help other Mastiffs in need.

Millie Spillers - Dacula, GA

SAMPSON'S JOURNEY

Cathy Goodison - Henryetta, Oklahoma

Kristi Everhart - Alma, Arizona

Diane Thornton - Little Rock, Arkansas

Brenda Boatright - Memphis, Tennesse

Tupelo, Mississippi

I'm home Mom

Millie Spiller - Dacula, Georgia

1. Mulligan

Mulligan was a therapy dog, certified by Therapy Dog International. He was my partner. He loved going to visit at nursing homes and special activities throughout the year.

Mulligan enjoyed everyone. Big or small, it didn't matter. If you talked to him, he was happy.

We visited a nursing home one time, and there was a teenage boy there who had been in an accident. He had severe brain damage and was partially paralyzed, with little use of his hands. He had been quiet since his accident, but when Mulligan walked up to his wheelchair, a huge smile crossed his face and his hand moved toward Mulligan. I helped him put his hand on Mulligan's head, and he laughed out loud. He was so happy! The nurse told me that was his first sound and the first time he had made an effort to reach for something. It was so heartwarming.

Each year there is a local fundraiser for Down syndrome research. It includes a walk around our local horse racing track, clowns, face painting, rides for the children, music, dancing, and t-shirt sales. Our therapy dog group visited there each year. Mulligan was always a huge hit with those with Down syndrome… young or old!

After our first visit on that great day, people remembered Mulligan. It was so wonderful to have people even remember his name, especially those with Down syndrome! One time there was a little girl with Downs who just adored Mulligan. She was about four or five years old. She just leaned up against him and put one arm over his back and wanted to stay there. In her precious little voice, she just kept saying, "I love you, Muddigan." I still tear up when I think of her. I'm so proud of his contribution to the people who met him!

Mulligan was what some call my "heart" dog. We had a connection like none I've ever had with any other dog. Mulligan has gone on to the Rainbow Bridge now and I miss him so much. He was truly a GREAT dog.
Judi Mott - Yukon, OK

2. Otis

Otis - I

When we moved to the farm, I decided it was time to indulge myself and finally get my first Mastiff. I wasn't new to dogs, and I had experience with a variety of breeds.

I had cared for my dad's dogs, my dogs, and relatives' dogs, so I was no stranger to the work and time a dog requires. What I hadn't expected, however, was for a dog to take care of me.

Having a special needs child is all-consuming. I do everything I can for her. Add a younger brother and a teenager into the mix, a marriage that is difficult at the best of times, a job that you go to and bring home with you, and there are never enough hours in the day to be everything for everyone. It becomes difficult some days to put one foot in front of the other. Setbacks seem more like mountains than the molehills they are. You find yourself wanting to give up.

Then a Mastiff comes into your life, and he just seems to know that reaching out for help seems impossible to you. Somehow he knows that you're doing everything you can to fight back the tears, and as he presses

2

his big head into your chest, he pushes just a little harder until you finally realize he wants to give you a hug.

Otis was amazing. I have loved all of the dogs that were a part of my life, mine or not, but I have never experienced the love of a dog such as a Mastiff.

When Otis was diagnosed with cardiomyopathy, a friend who is also a breeder, offered a pup to me. I accepted the generous offer and brought Hercules home in April 2010.

Even with his health declining, Otis mustered up the strength to keep up with Hercules.

In September 2010, I had to call Dr. Hawkins to the house. Otis had collapsed, and I could see it in his eyes he was saying goodbye. To this day, I cry when I think of him and his beautiful nature, his incredible love and his wonderful character. I am thankful each and every day for the time he gave Hercules because there are days when coping becomes an uphill battle, and I get that familiar nudge in my chest. Sometimes just for old times' sake, I hold off on the hug.

Otis - II

My daughter, Marissa, has Angelman syndrome. Every day brings challenges: physical, mental and emotional. I lost track of how many times people raised concerns about me getting a Mastiff. I heard it all.

Otis joined us when Marissa was two-and-a-half years old. Some of the best photos I have of Marissa have Otis in them. They made beautiful moments together.

I remember one photo in particular. Marissa had been playing with her bead maze, and Otis had lain down behind her offering a nice, warm support for her back. The kindness didn't go unnoticed; after Marissa had been playing for some time, she knocked her beads aside, turned around, and kissed Otis on the head. She had just learned how to kiss and it was definitely a moment I had to capture. Camera in hand, I prompted her to do it again, "Kiss-kiss, Marissa, kiss-kiss!" After a couple minutes of coaxing I saw her turn again, and as she leaned forward, I took several shots. One of the shots showed Otis getting a hug. We tried each and every time we kissed Marissa to show her a hug. She loved hugs, but could never seem to hug back. But she most definitely hugged Otis! His telltale groan of satisfaction said it all.

Over the four-and-a-half years that Otis shared with us, he had his jowls,

3

COMPILATION BY MILLIE SPILLERS

tail and ears pulled by Marissa. On occasion, we had to grab his tail from her as it was being guided to her open mouth. Not once did he ever complain. He loved her just as he loved the rest of us. He just seemed to know that she needed that extra patience and love.

Otis - III

Otis came to me as a pup at eight weeks old. He wasn't my first dog, but he was my first Mastiff.

Otis quickly became a member of the family. It wasn't unusual at all for a phone call to come in from the grandparents, and the "how is" roster to include Otis.

He was smart -- too smart sometimes. There wasn't a door that he couldn't master with some time and perseverance as my poor, frail, blind grandmother discovered when she was left alone in the kitchen while my mom took my daughter upstairs for bed. My mom assured and reassured my grandmother that she was completely safe; the dogs were all locked in the other room -- all 600 pounds of them!

A few moments passed and a familiar sound was heard. My grandmother may have been blind, but she wasn't deaf! Again the sound was heard. Now starting to get anxious, my grandmother started calling for my mom, because that sound she heard was the turning of a doorknob. The only response to her calls to my mom was another forceful turn of the doorknob, and then a bang. The door was open, and from the thuds of the heavy feet hitting the floor, my grandmother knew what and who were coming through the now open door. Isaac and Roxy, led by Otis, came prancing into the room.

She, to this day, gets this youthful awe in her voice when she tells us what happened next. As she sat quietly in the chair hoping not to be bumped, she felt something warm slide onto her lap. She put her hands out and felt the very large head of a dog. "He rested his head on my lap -- such a light head for such a big dog!"

The truth is that Otis' head was far from light. When my mom returned downstairs, she found my grandma still in the chair -- Otis standing in front -- Isaac and Roxy at his feet. Always the gentleman, he couldn't stand to see a lady left alone.
Sheri McIntosh - Moorefield, ON

3. Samson

Ten years ago, I had my very first English Mastiff. His name was Samson; he was fawn-colored, a beautiful and loving guy!

When he was two years old, my son had a baseball game, and although Samson loved attending the games, we left him at home. When we returned home, Samson was lying in the yard by the front porch. He had NEVER lain there. "Something must be wrong!" I yelled.

Imagine our surprise, however, when we found him curled around a newborn baby deer… its umbilical cord still attached! Samson ignored us; instead, he licked, cleaned and kept the fawn warm.

The baby deer was covered in creek mud, so we suspected she was born near the stream that is 500 yards from our house. Maybe she had been stuck in the mud until Samson rescued her and brought her home.

He was being a very good momma! I wrapped the baby in a towel and finished cleaning her. Not knowing what else to do, we took the baby to the town firehouse. We contacted the Wildcat Creek Wildlife Center in Delphi, Indiana, and one of the firemen agreed to transport the fawn to them.

A few days later, I received a phone call that the baby deer had a surrogate momma and was nursing. When she was old enough, they would release her onto their land.

Samson is the reason I am a Mastiff lover. He is the reason I have continued to own and rescue this wonderful breed of dog.
Holly Glidewell - Covington, IN

4. MAX

Part I, The Waxed Floor

After several attempts to make my wood floors look bright and shiny, I decided to use something other than Wood Wax. Why not try the same wax I use on the linoleum in the kitchen? It had always produced a bright and shiny look.

So while the family was away and Max was outside, I started putting the linoleum wax on the wood floors. It turned out beautifully. I then took Max for a walk while the floors dried.

When we returned home, the floors were dry. They looked great. I placed throw rugs on the newly waxed floor while in my bare feet. When I let Max in from the yard, he bolted for his favorite nap-time spot... on the opposite side of the wood floor.

Mayhem struck when Max hit the first throw rug. He sailed like riding on a magic carpet. Frightened, he jumped off the rug, landed on the waxed floor, and slid into a spread eagle. Unthinking, I ran to him, hit one of the other rugs, sailed across the floor, and landed on my rearend.

Max belly-crawled to safe carpeting. I lay on my newly waxed floor, looking up at the ceiling, trying to figure out what had just happened. I carefully stood and nearly went down again. I had turned my beautiful, shiny wood floors into a nightmarish death trap!

Max was so traumatized that he was trying to hide his huge body under our bed, but only his head would fit... and that's how I found him. I felt horrible, both for him and my rearend!

While in the bedroom comforting Max, my daughter came home. Seeing the floors had been waxed, she removed her shoes, and as soon as her socks hit the floor, she went airborne.

Once we were safe together on the carpet, we decided that the wax wasn't going away for a long time, because I did such a good job of putting it on nice and thick.

I crawled across the waxed floor to the basement, found a box of sandpaper, and my daughter and I sanded the entire floor.

It took Max a long time to walk on the wood floors again after his magic carpet had turned into such a fiasco.

Part II, Intruder

Max is very shy; his first name was Shylo before I adopted him. He is very gentle, even though he had little human contact as a pup; therefore, it did take time for him to warm up to us.

He seldom barks. I know he would never hurt anyone, but his mere size is a warning to anyone who knows I live alone. In fact, he's so gentle that backyard squirrels pay him no mind. He's even leery of neighborhood "ankle-biter" dogs.

On one particular night, I heard him barking and growling. He was fixated on the backyard; the hair stood on his back and his tail was raised. I can tell you I was really scared! I turned on the yard light. The back gate was open, the patio screen had been cut, and there were beer cans on the ground. Max wanted out, but I kept him with me.

The police checked out the neighborhood but could not find anyone. One officer told me, "With a dog that size, I don't think you have to worry about intruders."

Max is my hero. He had sensed the prowlers, knew something was wrong, and had sounded the alarm.

Still, he barks at anything that is unusual to him: a falling tree limb or a garbage can blown over in the wind. Last Christmas I was walking him during the evening, and he started barking at a nativity scene -- how embarrassing!

He is older now and his sight is not as good as it used to be, but I still praise him when he barks. He just wants to be sure that I'm safe. He will always protect me… and I will do the same for him.

Nancy Rosa - Grand Rapids, MI

5. Whiskey River

© 2011 • Jen Geraghty
www.TriPodDogDesign.com

Steve and I were coming in the back door of our kitchen with groceries, when the large dog we were watching decided to attack Steve without warning. Something about seeing Steve carrying bags triggered the attack. This dog weighed about 130 or so. He knocked the groceries out of Steve's arms and bit his left forearm.

Whiskey was standing in the kitchen next to me, and I had my back to the door. We heard Steve say "NO!" and Whiskey sprang into action and bit the dog so that he would let go of Steve. The dog turned his attention toward Whiskey, and the two of them latched onto each other. The snarling and fighting was intense.

Their fight lasted only about four minutes, but it seemed like an eternity with me and Steve both trying to pull the dogs apart, and us both slipping and sliding in the growing pool of blood from Steve's arm dripping onto the kitchen floor. I had a hold on the collar of the other dog, and Steve had Whiskey. Whiskey obeyed when we commanded him to stop fighting, but the other dog would not relent. I tried everything I could think of, from yelling at the dog to gouging his eyes with my fingers, to get him to stop fighting. We could not get the dog to let go of Whiskey's ear whatsoever. Nothing helped.

Finally I got an idea to give the smaller dog a hockey-style hip check and bodyslam him up against the kitchen island. I did that as hard as I could, and smashed his head against the cabinet. He released Whiskey and bit me in the thigh, but I didn't realize that I'd been bitten with all the excitement of the moment. I dragged him to his wire crate and locked him in it.

Steve led Whiskey out the back door to check him for wounds and found none, miraculously, and there were no wounds on the other dog either. We called animal control to come and get the vicious dog. I finally noticed that I was bleeding, and Steve left me at home to wait for animal control to arrive (because he had to go to the E.R. for medical assistance immediately). He got X-rays to make sure no bones were broken, and got six stitches in a deep laceration on the base of the thumb; there were several puncture wounds that needed attention.

If Whiskey had not been there to stop the attack, with the strength that dog had, he would have been easily able to knock Steve down and maul him horribly, perhaps kill him. Whiskey really truly is a hero, and risked his life to save his family.

Afterward, Whiskey would not let us out of his sight, making sure that we were safe. When the grandchildren came over for a visit the following weekend, he let the two-year-old climb all over him, wagging his tail like crazy. He has a heart of gold and adores his family.
Tina Knepper-Smith - Belleville, IL

6. Indy Anna

More than a brindle babysitter, not quite a show dog, still Indy is a true mascot of the Mastiff breed when it comes to her devotion to her family.

Indy helped teach our son to walk. If he fell, she would lie next to him, and slowly sit up when he was ready to get back up on his feet. Then, she would walk with him as he clutched a handful of her skin. They have had many adventures together.

One adventure I will never forget:

We were out raking the yard: my son, Indy, my husband and I. The neighbor drives in, pulls up next to our yard and shut off her truck. When she starts up her truck, Indy stepped in front of us three and wouldn't budge a step away from us. Indy then started leaning against our son, guiding him backwards.

I will never be able to find another Indy; money could never replace her. Indy and my son are one month and twelve days apart.
Amber M. Stevens - Northwood, IO

7. The Duke

The day we brought our Duke home, he immediately bonded with the family, especially our one-year-old twin boys. They were inseparable buddies from the start. We have a big Italian family and were having a family dinner.

Everyone was getting ready to leave and the front door was continuously being opened and closed. I was in the kitchen cleaning up and saying my goodbyes to everyone. One minute there are the sounds of goodnight and goodbyes from all, and the next, a bone-chilling scream.

My mother was stumbling up the walkway with one of our twin sons Wyatt in her arms screaming, "I almost ran over the baby!" I stood in the middle of the kitchen frozen with fear. My husband ran out and took Wyatt from her arms. He was fine, thank God.

You see, the twins hate it when there Noni leaves, and so Wyatt followed her out the door, but was lost in all the commotion. When my mom went to back out of the driveway, she was stopped by the furious barking and sheer size of our Mastiff, Duke. He was behind her car in the driveway with Wyatt. Not only did he put himself in between the car and the baby to protect him, he barked in warning to try to get my mom to stop.

When my mom got out of her car, she was a little frustrated with Duke and said, "What are you doing out here? You know you aren't allowed out the front door without permission." He just stood his ground, and when my mom looked behind him, there was Wyatt holding onto Duke's tail crying. My mom was so overwhelmed with the fear of what almost happened, she just started screaming. My mom picked Wyatt up and started for the house with Duke trotting dutifully beside her, keeping watch over his baby.

We all started crying and hugging Duke and praising him. Poor guy was looking at us like, "What are you all fussing about; I just did my duty." Duke had a steak dinner that night and slept with the twins. Duke was only nine months old at the time and already a hero.
Jenny Reed - Sparks, NY

8. Conan

It was around February of 1990 when I brought home a five-and-a-half-week-old fawn Mastiff, Conan of Christmas Dawn. There were four others living in my home in addition to Conan and me: my four-year-old daughter, my two teenage step-kids, and my husband. While we were all on board with my new puppy, the dynamics in the family were a mess. I was 29 then and my husband, as yet undiagnosed, was a multiple personality.

Conan only lived long enough to save my life. He was gentle, well mannered, fun loving, and he turned into a giant glee-filled joy-bomb. One of his favorite antics was to bolt out the door and into the neighborlady's home when he got wind of her standing in her doorway. We would have to race over and collect him. He loved all of us, but I belonged to him.

I wasn't sleeping at night. I feared my husband and thought I wouldn't wake up. There's no attractive way to tell that part of the story. While my days being a mother, loving my job, and training a new pup were wonderful distractions that kept me in the dark (a blissful state of denial) about other things, my home was not right; and while I felt it, I couldn't believe my gut was telling me the truth. I was afraid I wouldn't wake up in the mornings. I was shrouded with a veil of disbelief at my own life, and denial kept me blind to the truth.

After my husband would begin to breathe evenly, I would go to the study and sit up, nearly all night. Conan sat behind me with his huge head on my shoulder. This happened for many months. I was numb with fear, and often sobbed for hours. At the time, of course, I couldn't define what was happening. I didn't have this hindsight.

One evening, my husband lunged at me and grabbed my throat, unexpectedly and quickly. In a blink, Conan had him on the ground, flat with his mouth over my husband's neck, growling low and controlled. At this point, Conan was about 180 pounds and had never shown aggression; and in fact, even then he seemed quite in control of the situation. I and my husband both were stunned, and when he laughed nervously and said, "Okay Conan, get off." Conan stepped in closer. He let my husband go when I pulled him off. This act brought home what was happening. The time it took gave me pause to "see" my life. I suspect this is the sort of thing only someone who loves and is abused can understand.

I left, and divorced, this man within months of this event. He is now in prison for other crimes. I found, then, a tiny efficiency apartment for my daughter and I; and while I looked for the seemingly non-existent place that would allow a 200-pound dog, Conan stayed with my brother and his family. Immediately Conan began to lose weight and turn yellow. After numerous visits to the vet, and nearly 100 pounds of weight lost, I said goodbye to my precious ward. He had been suffering from cancer, and the loss of my dog left me nearly immobile for weeks. Even today, over 25 years later as I write this, I cry thinking of my own loss. I don't recall grieving so heavily, and yet not completely, over anyone, which is annoying to non-dog-loving people. I have owned many dogs and loved them all, but I have no doubt that his short life saved my own, and I suppose I feel a bit cheated out of being able to reward him with the life he deserved.

Conan passed away on an air mattress with fans on him in the intensive care unit of our local university veterinary care center, surrounded by a few young students. My grief was overwhelming. Seeing him at the end of his very short life, symbolized the beginning of my own new life alone with my young daughter. I cannot think of his eyes on me without many tears, even today. While I am today an old cynic, and do not believe in miracles beyond walking on grass, and love; if I am wrong, then Conan was certainly sent to me to be my angel for that short period of time, and to get me out safely.

So in 2009, with my daughter grown and moved away, and my pennies saved, I bought a beautiful home. I had fantasized many times of bringing home another Mastiff, but I always managed to talk myself out of loving something that much again.

Three days after moving into my home, I was surprised by an unwanted male stranger in my window who attempted to scare me. I suspect he was on drugs by the way he strolled off when I shrieked hysterical profanity at him. Perhaps, if one is not as cynical as I am, he too was a messenger sent to me. I took a day off work, picked up a news paper, drove to a neighboring town, and placed a six-week-old brindle puppy into my lap.

Doubting my own sanity (as I sometimes do), I phoned my daughter, "What the heck am I doing?"

My daughter said, "Jesus Christ, Mom, what has taken you so long?"

So Viggo, my 170-pound still-growing brindle Mastiff, who is not sure if he should chase or run from bunnies (and squirrels startle him), is not Conan. But when we take walks after work, he will not allow a man to approach me (he is formidable looking, but strangers don't know his greatest terror would be having to bite anyone or anything). He is clearly not an incarnation of Conan. He is skittish, doubtful, inhibited, and a bit of a puss. But I love him not one bit less than I did Conan, my beautiful fawn Mastiff. I have owned two other dogs since the passing of Conan; and before Viggo, one poundpup stayed with me for seventeen years, "loved them both" of course.

Viggo will be my last canine. Since bringing him into my home, I have become once again, aware of how love holds one hostage. The responsibility to keep another heartbeat as free of suffering as one can is a taxing chore, but the payoff is worth it. I worry during my vacations. I take him with me when I go shopping, so he can smell fresh air from the car window and slime up my car. I daily walk him through crowds to try and desensitize him of his nervous fear of people. I give children treats to give to him so he will love them, instead of trying to hide under my ass. I have to vacuum daily. My sofa smells like Mastiff ass. My daughter claims my car does also. And I still wonder why I waited so long to bring home another Mastiff. I come home from work and he flips onto his back in joy; he tries to speak in a human voice. When my boyfriend comes home from work, Viggo is a giant glee-filled joy-bomb, leaping into the air in an attempt to demonstrate to my partner how loved he is. Everyone should be loved like that.
Joy Richardson

9. The Nature of the Beast

Introduction

After visiting with my in-laws one Sunday afternoon, my husband and I stopped at a local fruit stand to pick up some fresh Georgia peaches. I also took a free hunting newsletter, not my typical read, but my Nook was dead and I needed something for the two-hour ride home. How was I to know what an amazing story was inside this little gazette? After reading "The Nature of the Beast," I couldn't wait to get home and contact the author. This story was a perfect example of a Mastiff's gentle nature, and I had to have it for my book. I contacted the paper, gave them my phone number and anxiously waited for the author to call. He responded promptly, and I was bouncing with questions, "Where's this sweet dog? How's the little girl?" When I finally took a breath, DaWayne said, "It's just a short story I wrote; it's not true." He said he didn't really know anything about English Mastiffs, had only seen one at a dog show. I told him it was amazing how well he described the true nature of a Mastiff, and one would have responded just that way in the scenario. The story is fiction, but the meaning could not be truer.
Millie Spillers - Dacula, GA

10. The Nature of the Beast

"Are you sure that he is in there?" asked Ted Franklin.

"Yep," answered Gil Timmins, "got a sighting of ol' Houdini yesterday evening, not far from the state park."

Houdini was a mountain of a wild hog that seems to have more lives than two litters of cats. Every time that someone has been able to bay him, the monster pig has escaped. If the catch dogs even got their chance, Houdini made short use of them leaving dogs strewn in his wake.

"Is Roddy bringing her?" continued Gil.

"I talked to him a bit ago," answered Ted, "It took some doing to get her in that travel box. Sheba can be a little testy at times."

"I imagine," said Gil with a bit of a put-on shiver.

Roddy Nettles and his brother Gary arrived a few minutes later with a huge homemade dog box in the back of their truck. As the truck stopped, a deep grumbling noise slipped from the welded steel dog carrier. Ted and Gil stepped back instinctively.

The plan was to (if the wind was right) push the hogs away from the state park, and hope that Houdini and the rest will move toward an old hay field that is above a rather large high-water wash and ravine. If the dogs bayed, and it was Houdini, they would give Sheba her chance.

The wind was in their favor with a chance of thundershowers later; so once it got dark, Ted and Gil let loose Gidget, Burt and JoJo, three of the best bay dogs in the county. It was not long before JoJo struck a fresh trail and was off to the races, baying that soulful electric sound that all hog hunters love to hear. Gidget and Burt joined in on the chorus. Ted and Gil had radio collars on their dogs and were following the progress on a special GPS program along with Roddy and Gary in Gil's truck.

"Do you reckon its Houdini?" asked Roddy.

"Hard to tell," replied Ted. "JoJo sounds awfully wound up though."

After about 15 minutes, the dogs suddenly bayed. The woods were exploding with the dogs' frantic barking and growling and ear-shattering pig squeals. "They bayed!" shouted Gary.

"They're down close to the old mill road," said Gil looking up from his laptop. "Roddy, you and Gary can drive almost right there. Need to get Sheba in close as we can if we need her! Me and Ted are going to cut straight through!"

"Let's roll!" shouted Gary. And the race was on...

Ted and Gil got there first. At the base of a blown-down oak, three dogs did their dance whirling in and out keeping the biggest hog either Ted or Gil had ever seen pinned to the huge root base of the tree. "It's Houdini!" exclaimed Gil.

Ted was already on his cell phone, "Roddy, bring Sheba and hurry!"

Ted and Gil were doing their best to keep Burt, Gidget and JoJo safe from the vicious swirling tusker. JoJo was bleeding from a gash in his side. Gidget's left ear was shredded.

A light shone entering the small opening in the woods. It was Gary and Roddy, and between them on a choker chain was a big black dog that stood nearly to their hip. Sheba was part Mastiff and parts something big and nasty. Beside her bad temperament and ill nature, she was perhaps the best pure catch dog there has ever been.

"Boys," shouted Roddy, "grab your dogs!"

Ted and Gil scrambled to get a leash on their dogs as Sheba broke free from Gary's grasp.

The big black dog hit Houdini in full stride like a linebacker hitting a quarterback on a blindside blitz. The two crashed and tumbled through the brush. The hog had nearly three times Sheba's mass, but what she lacked in weight, Sheba made up for with pure animal rage.

The men tried to keep up with the rampaging behemoths. Their head lanterns caught glimpses of flashing tusks and gnashing teeth through the underbrush. Suddenly, Houdini slipped and Sheba latched on the big hog's right ear. "She's got him now!" shouted Roddy, as he reached into his shoulder bag and grabbed some heavy nylon cord.

It was then that the impossible happened. Houdini broke free. With a lunge, he exploded into the thicket behind him and plunged headlong into the deep ravine that stretched across that section of the woods, with Sheba dead on his heels and the big hog's bloody, shredded ear in her mouth.

Cindy was a simply wonderful child of four years of age. The shoulder length ringlets of her blonde hair framed eyes of emerald green. A light-blue barrette that looked like the wings of a butterfly was clipped in the back. She had a smile so infectious that even the butterflies that would gather in her mother's flower garden would pause in absolute amazement when she chased after them. Everything would be perfect in little Cindy's world if it were not for her being born deaf due to her mother contracting Cytomegalovirus, or CMV, during her pregnancy. Being deaf from birth, Cindy has never spoken a single word. Cindy's parents, Joyce and Gregory Hartford, both loved the outdoors which brought them to F.D. Roosevelt State Park that weekend. Listening to the birds, walking the trails, and watching Cindy ramble after the butterflies, were just a few of the things they loved to do.

"I am going up to that roadside stand," shout Gregory as he headed toward his truck. "I want some more of that sweet corn on the grill tonight."

"Sounds good to me," replied Joyce as she hung a few handwashed clothes on a makeshift clothes line, "and get some strawberries for Cindy."

Joyce looked out the window to check on Cindy just in time to see her heading toward the treeline, chasing after a particularly large yellow butterfly. In her haste to get Cindy's attention, Joyce slipped while exiting their travel trailer's door, and fell and hit her head on the makeshift steps. Enamored with fluttering yellow wings, Cindy never saw her mother fall or the blood trickling from her temple. She just followed the butterfly deeper and deeper into the trees.

Gregory took a little longer than he expected at the roadside produce stand. He met a park ranger who was also buying some corn. They had discussed with vigor, the virtues of corn being placed directly on the grill as opposed to slathering it in butter and wrapping it in aluminum foil first. When Gregory arrived back at the campsite, he looked on in horror as he found his wife unconscious and bleeding on the ground, with Cindy nowhere to be found. Luckily, the park ranger gave him his card at the produce stand. As he rushed to his unmoving wife, he frantically dialed his number.

After hearing his cries for help, some people who were camping down a ways rushed to see what was happening.

"Help my wife!" Gregory exclaimed. "I got to find my daughter!" Cindy's father stood up, and with his heart beating in his throat, frantically looked left and right. Gregory did not know which way to go first. It was then that he spied the little blue barrette at the treeline. He raced into the woods screaming Cindy's name. It did not matter that he knew she could not hear him. It just made him scream louder.

It was nearing dark when the ranger and a group of others finally caught up with him. Exhausted, dirty, and bleeding from scratches on his face and arms, Gregory fell to his knees sobbing. "Joyce?" asked Gregory in a voice laden with despair.

"She's headed to the county hospital," replied the ranger. "I am sure she'll be just fine."

"Go get some lights," the ranger shouted back over his shoulder. "Buddy, we are going to find your little girl if it takes all night."

The moon was nearly full. It cast an ethereal glow throughout the forest. The air was turning cooler. Cindy sniffed and rubbed her now runny nose with back of her hand. The pretty flower-covered sun dress her mommy had dressed her in this morning was covered in dirt and grime. The barrette that held her blonde hair was gone. Her green eyes shone through the cascade of yellow hair mixed with pine straw, leaves, and grass.

Suddenly in the brush directly in front of her, something very large and hairy emerged. The smell of feces, rotten earth, and blood filled the air. Breathing like a freight train, Houdini snorted and stepped toward Cindy. Startled, she stumbled and fell against a small cropping of trees.

It was then that a huge, black, growling mass exploded from the brush, catching the huge hog full-on. The impact sent both creatures sprawling. Sheba, tattered and bleeding, was first to her feet. Houdini loosened a primal noise that was more roar than squeal. Cindy's eyes widened as she watched the two behemoths size each other up one more time. Sheba dove in, but only to be caught by a wave of Houdini's huge head, and was tossed aside. One of his three-inch tusks ripped Sheba's foreleg in the process. Sheba, never slowing, regained her footing and attacked again. This time there was an opening.

Instead of grabbing the ear like she did last time, her gaping mouth clamped down on Houdini right where the base of the jaw meets the throat. Her teeth were set in flesh and bone. Sheba was not going to let go this time. The two flipped over into the bushes out of Cindy's line of sight. It was good that Cindy could not hear the guttural carnage and death throes that ensued.

Cindy's eyes strained to see through the moonlit trees and brush. Confused and not knowing what had just happened, she sat there cold, hungry, and very scared. Slowly, a large black figure came into view. Limping, bleeding, breathing hard and labored, Sheba cocked her massive head at the child.

Cindy recognized what Sheba was. The lady that lived next door to them had a big black Labrador retriever. She remembered how she reached out and the dog would sniff her hand then lick it. Cindy stood up slowly, and as Sheba eased closer, she reached out to the injured creature. Sheba had never seen anything like this. She sensed no danger; so out of natural curiosity, Sheba sniffed Cindy's hand. The smell triggered something that was buried deep inside Sheba. She licked the small child's hand. As Cindy reached and gently stroked the side of Sheba's head, Sheba returned the gesture with a sloppy lick to the side of Cindy's head.

Sheba's legs suddenly became wobbly. From blood loss and exhaustion, Sheba could not stand any longer. She lay down at Cindy's feet and closed her eyes. Instinctively, Cindy did the same. Curling up next to the huge dog, Cindy was warm and not scared anymore. She also closed her eyes and dreamed of butterflies and of her mommy.

Ted, Roddy, Gil, and Gary had heard of the lost little girl and had pitched in on the search. They would look for Sheba later. They had regrouped back at the main highway to reevaluate their game plan. Gregory looked like a car wreck. Everyone was worse for wear.

It was then that the ambulance showed up and the rear doors opened, and Joyce Hartford (bandaged head and all) stepped out. "Joyce!" shouted Gregory as he ran to his wife. "What are you doing here?"

"I'm all right," she said. "Cindy? Have you found her? Do you know where she is?"

Before the distraught father could answer, a call came in across the walkie-talkie. "We found her," came across the air, "and you aren't going to believe this."

The group led by Gregory and Joyce hurriedly followed the directions given. They arrived at a small opening in the woods. Everyone stood in absolute amazement at what they saw waiting on them.

There was Cindy, sound asleep, curled up next to the biggest dog anyone of them had ever seen. The big black dog which looked like it had been in a war, had its huge head raised. A deep rumbling growl permeated the area. "Whoa," said Gary, "that's Sheba."

The four hog hunters quickly told the story of earlier that night. "I got to get my daughter away from that monster!" shouted Gregory as he headed toward Sheba and Cindy.

"Look over there," said Roddy, as he pointed his flashlight at a giant hog piled up in the edge of the brush with a gaping hole in its neck.

"I wouldn't if I was you," said Gil while stopping Gregory with his hand. "We don't want to upset her."

It was then that Joyce shot past both men. "Joyce!" exclaimed Gregory. "What are you doing!"

"Getting my daughter," stated Joyce. She slowly approached Sheba and Cindy. No one in the group moved a muscle or seemed to even breathe. The growling from Sheba deepened and grew louder as Joyce got closer.

"Listen girl," spoke Joyce in a soft teary-eyed voice, while extending her hand palm-up toward the huge black dog, "I just want my baby."

Sheba stopped growling and sniffed the air. She cocked her head slightly. When Joyce was close enough, Sheba nuzzled Cindy's hair, then leaned out and licked Joyce's hand. "That's a good girl," said Joyce as she gently stroked the side of Sheba's head, just as Cindy had done a few hours earlier.

Cindy's eyes slowly opened. A smile appeared on her dirt-smudged face and she jumped to her mother's arms. Joyce gathered Cindy into her arms, turned, and began walking back to the group. Sheba then, still on wobbly legs, stood and began walking at Joyce's side. Joyce looked down. Joyce and Sheba's eyes met. The big dog's foreleg began to trickle blood as she walked. Sheba began to growl as the unlikely threesome approached the on-watching group of disbelieving men, which parted like the Red Sea to let them through.

As Joyce passed her husband, she said four words: "Get me a vet."

As the sun began to rise, the group of men stood in awe of what they had just witnessed.

"I ain't never seen the likes of it," said Ted.

"Reckon," asked Gary, "it's because they are all female?"

"Nope," answered Gil. "I believe it is just the nature of the beast."

A year later, Joyce stuck her head out of the little travel trailer door which was parked at a campground on Jekyll Island and shouted, "Sheba! Get Cindy. It's lunch time!"

Both Joyce and Gregory watched with smiling faces as a huge black dog playfully corralled the little girl who was, as usual, chasing butterflies, and herded her toward the little trailer and lunch.
DaWayne Spires - Kathleen, GA

11. Sampson My Hero

I rescued Sampson almost one year ago, and we bonded immediately. One week ago, I adopted Britt, a two-year-old fluffy Mastiff. She was not a rescue, just a beautiful pampered girl that needed a new home.

She is such a sweet girl, but very timid and not accustomed to my loud, kid-filled house. On her second day here, she bolted from the yard and ended up in my neighbor's thicket of briars and kudzu. Poor baby was stuck and scared to move. Sampson rushed in beside her and made a path; she followed him out, up the hill, and home.

Day five, she ran again, and this time further down the neighborhood. She ran into an overgrown area which had a creek below. Only her head appeared above the mighty growth; it looked like "Where's Waldo!!"

Once again she would not move, so my husband ran home and got Sampson. With his gentle loving nature, he coaxed her out and brought her home. I think because Sampson is a rescue, he appreciates the life he has now. He doesn't yearn for more and is able to think of others instead of himself.

That which does not kill us only makes us stronger, and Sampson is a pillar of strength. I thank God everyday for the many volunteers that

brought him to me. I love my Sammy boy.
Millie Spillers - Dacula, GA

12. Morgan

Last night's bloat took our sweet Morgan, better known as Morgie Porgy.

Morgan was a little on the shy side, a real homebody and so, so sweet. Morgan was our tattletale; she never did anything bad, but would come and tell us when another dog was getting into trouble.

She was always in bed at eight o'clock; and if all the other dogs were not in bed at that time, she would come out of her room and talk to us, telling us it was time everyone went to bed. She had her routine and knew the house rules, and found it of great concern if her routine was broken or if some dog broke the rules. Because of this, Morgan never got in any trouble; we will miss her bedtime announcements.

Quite often we would be watching TV after eight o'clock, and Morgan would come out of her bedroom and give a little speech that sounded like, "Wo, wowo, wo wo." Then my husband and I would talk back to her, and she would carry on the "wowo" conversation until we got up and put the other dogs to bed. I will miss our little conversations.

If her bad sister Bella was doing something bad, which was quite often,

Morgan would come to us and give us the "wowo" talk, and we would know to go and see what Bella was up to. It was quite funny that she was a tattletale, but we loved her lots. We will miss you Morgan.
Sharon Medforth - Ladysmith, British Columbia

13. Rhea

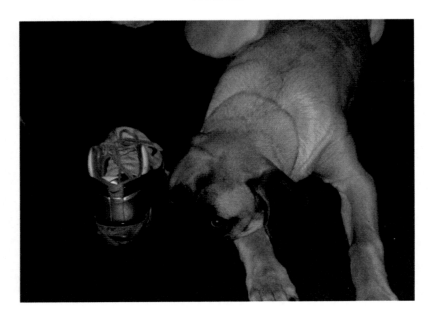

My boyfriend's mom, sister, and niece came over to see our new house yesterday. Jeff's niece is almost 18 months old and has cerebral palsy. I was AMAZED at how gentle Rhea was with her. The only child she's been around since I've had her was my nephew (also 18 months), and she pushed him down into a corner and licked him. But with Taylor (the niece) she just walked over, set her head on Jeff's sister's arm, and let Taylor pet her. I don't know if it's because Taylor was sitting on someone's lap (although I was holding my nephew and she still licked him to death). Maybe she knew that there was something different about her... I don't know. It was really awesome to watch this dog (that is ALL puppy around people) be as calm and gentle as can be with that child.
Brittany R. Udelhofen

14. Miss Patience

This is a true story about a wonderful Mastiff with the ability to heal a broken heart. Before I can tell you the story, I need to explain how I came to meet this charming Miss Patience.

I have had a Mastiff in my life for over 10 years. My Mastiffs have been my constant companions and were trained to be Therapy/Service Dogs.

Miss Ali worked with Hospice and was the stand-in for the remedial readers who loved the "Mudge" series. Ali attended over 80 deaths, helping those who were actively dying to pass peacefully while they held onto her. Ali left me five years ago due to a systemic infection.

Oscar was a true hospital employee. He loved working with brain injury patients and those on ventilators. My Oscar left me May 6, 2008, due to a severe spinal cord illness. That brings me to my broken heart. Oscar was my heart and soul. He never left my side, and when it was time to let him go to the Bridge, I thought my heart would never heal.

A local Mastiff owner (MC Kay) contacted me to tell me about her new litter of puppies, and to tell me that if I thought it might help, I was welcome to come for a visit. I took that trip and was happily surrounded by a living room full of beautiful, healthy puppies.

It happened that one of the pups had a stomach upset and had to go to the vet to be checked out. During the time the baby was at the vet, I was also privileged to meet Ron, who is the two-legged dad, and is a dear man who loves puppy breath as much as I do. I stayed behind to smell the puppy breath and keep an eye on the crew. I noticed that Mama Patience was watching me through the screen door as I wiped little butts and cleaned up several of the tee-tale brown poops. Each time I picked up one of her pups, I reassured her that I would take good care. She seemed to know I was trustworthy but watched me nonetheless. I had no way of knowing she was reading my sadness.

When MC (the owner, who herself is a most remarkable person) returned home with the little one who had a bad case of gas but was feeling much better, the puppies were taken outside for their afternoon romp. MC and I went out to sit in the yard with the babies, their mom, and their aunt Seri (Miniature Schnauzer). As soon as I sat down, Miss Patience came over to me and put her beautiful head in my lap to let me know she knew how much I missed Oscar. I hugged her and told her about Oscar. As the tears streamed down my face, she licked them away and rubbed her cheek on my cheek the way Oscar did to comfort me. It was uncanny. She stayed with me the entire time I was in the backyard, except for the times MC called her to show me her rally training. But as soon as she was released by her mom, she came straight back to me. She gave and gave, knowing how deeply I needed to be the recipient of that special Mastiff understanding.

As I got ready to leave and stood up, she leaned on me very gently and I could feel her say, "You'll be alright. It will still hurt, but Oscar is watching over you." I don't know if that really is what she said, but I choose to believe she did. I wanted to tell you about this amazing girl because she exemplifies what a Mastiff is. Those of us who have been privileged to have one of these magnificent creatures in our lives know this is what the Mastiff breed is all about. Thank you, Miss Patience, because without you I don't think my heart could have started to heal. I love you sweet girl.

Toni Leah Bush - Brewster, MA

15. Soko

My husband had always wanted a Mastiff; I was a Lab person myself. So I spent over a year researching the breed, looking up all the negatives, and weighing them against the positives. After almost two years, I decided that the breed seemed PERFECT... Sure there was slobber and fur, but I have four kiddos so slobber, hair, pee, poop, and whatever else you can dream up are not a HUGE issue. Ha!

Anyway, on December 6, I went and picked up our nine-week-old Soko, and he has been a dream ever since. He slept all night in his crate the first night without a sound.

He has never chewed on anything much besides his toys. (Stuffed animals and pillows are a favorite, so we just make sure those are out of reach.)

He passed his CGC at a mere seven months, and has perfect house manners with just a few outbreaks of the crazies here and there.

But seriously, the LOVE he has brought to us, is soooo much MORE than any problems we have ever had with him. The way he looks at us with those big soft brown eyes, as if to say, "YOU ALL ARE MY FAVORITE THINGS."

The way when I am cooking or doing anything, he is just right there near me, lying in the floor, or just sitting and watching. The way he is soooo very gentle with the two-year-old, and watches over him as if he were his own pup... The way he knows each of the children, and how rough and tumble he can be with them. He knows my daughter (six-year-old) is petite and not a toughie like her older brothers, so he uses her as a snuggle-buddy.

But especially here lately how he just knows when one of us needs a hug, or some nuzzling. How he just walks up and puts his big soft muzzle in your lap, or nudges your hand with that big soft nose and runs his head under so you HAVE to pet him. If you are sitting in the floor, the way he just walks up, face to face with you and puts his chin on your shoulder to give you a hug with a gentle nuzzle as if to say, "HERE I AM, LEAN ON ME..."

He has such a quiet, gentle, peaceful, wise spirit. I don't know if it is true of all Mastiffs, but from what I read, it seems to be the norm.

He is so good to strangers young-and-old, cats, dogs, and everyone. (Cats are fun to chase sometimes though, ha ha... they move...) I have taken him to the school for field days, to ball games, to MANY crowded places, and for a crowd of six-year-olds, he will lie down and just eat up the love, never once acting as if he is being annoyed...

The most precious thing we have witnessed was last spring. He was just about six months old (but a beast already), and I took him to the school for field day. The second grade class came out; he was eating up the attention, sitting there so sweetly and lovingly.

Up walks a little boy with some physical and mental challenges. He wanted to pet Soko, but all the others were gathered all around Soko. Soko looked over and saw this boy and gently got up, walked to him, and sat right beside him so the boy could pet him. The boy hugged and hugged on Soko and bragged and bragged how much Soko loved him. Soko just put his head on the boy's shoulder and nuzzled him ever so gently. They were best friends for an hour and more. Soko never left this boy's side after that. All the other kids came and went petting and loving Soko, but Soko was drawn to this particular child. This boy was loving it, and just sooo excited. It was the sweetest thing ever. I don't even have the words to describe how it made this little boy feel and how many adults commented on what an awesome dog Soko was. This boy's aide, his teacher, and his mother were awed, and in love too. They said this boy NEVER came out of his shell this much...

Anyway, as I sit here with the big giant head in my lap, nudging my hand so that I don't forget to scratch here or there, I am just in AWE of what an AMAZING breed our Gentle Giants are.

My husband is constantly saying how we will NEVER be without a Mastiff again. I can't imagine our house without our precious boy.

Even my big stubborn-mule macho husband has shed a tear over the fact that the life span of these angels is so very short; and that our baby who was just one-and-a-half years old when Soko came to live with us, will never know not having Soko, and will probably just be a preteen when Soko is called on to be a guardian angel on the other side. It breaks our heart and makes us realize that life is too short. But even more, how precious the past eight-and-a-half months with Soko have been! I mean a mere eight-and-a-half months and he has brought such joy, such fun, and SO MUCH LOVE. I can't imagine how much he can bring in ten or more years.

Snoring, slobber, gas, and fur... bring it on, because the LOVE OF A MASTIFF is worth SO MUCH MORE.
Heather Kiser

16. Monte

I am lucky enough to live with and enjoy Monte. Monte had exhibited nurturing/nursing tendencies even as a very young dog. While Edward, his same-age flashy Mastiff show dog, zoomed around the show rings, Monte was busy loving and kissing older folks and children in wheel chairs -- thus finding his niche in life.

It was Kim Morrell who informed me about therapy dogs as her Mastiff, Harry, set unbelievable numbers of hours and visits as a TDI volunteer. The New England Mastiff Club held CGC and TDI testing at their first gathering, and I decided to give Monte a shot. He passed all testing and thus his therapy dog career began.

He has worked weekly as the Library Dog with Children's Hour, marched in many parades with livestock surrounding him, and most importantly, has worked with Hospice and many ill people, providing comfort in their last hours on earth. He has attended very large meetings of Hospice workers, providing love and nurturing to these hard workers who care for the terminally ill.

Just recently, Monte stayed with a dying resident in the nursing home he volunteers at, resting his big soft head on her bed, kissing her hand, and bringing a peaceful smile to her face. This woman had no relatives or friends to be with her at the end. My mother used to say to me, "No one should die alone." What is the value of this wonderful dog?

Monte works weekly in a nursing home/assisted-living facility and visits the memory care unit with residents who have dementia. Just a few weeks ago, as one resident was talking to Monte, another resident was on the floor kissing his feet and body, loving and hugging him. This was a resident who rarely came out of her shell, but now exhibited such joy, by touching and loving this big dog.

The oldest resident of the town I live in was nearing to her final time on earth, and Monte was asked to be there with her. Since she was 102, she outlived her family; and though in and out of consciousness, I am quite certain she felt his presence and comfort.

Having had many prestigious show wins with many of my Mastiffs, I can tell you that with the heart and soul that Monte shares by providing joy and comfort to those that are most in need, he is the biggest winner of all.
Roberta Pavoll - Mt. Vernon, NH

17. Ben

My story of devotion may be a little bit different than others. You see, Ben hasn't had to protect me from anything or anyone, nor has he ever had to put his life on the line for me. But, Ben has "saved" me.

I picked Ben up six months after I'd said goodbye to my Bull Mastiff that I'd had for eleven years. I was heartbroken.

Ben had huge pawprints to fill, and I wasn't expecting him to even come close. Boy, did he prove me wrong!

Ben is the absolute love of my life. He is the most gentle, loving guy who has never met anyone or anything he doesn't like. I never have to look far to find him, as he's usually touching me in some way all of the time!

Ben has turned into so much more than I'd ever dreamed he would. He's my walking partner, my BIG lapdog, a great listener, and he always makes me proud when we meet new people.

When I think of what true devotion means, I think of this big, lovable Mastiff named Ben who makes me smile every day.
Donna Sawyer - Bucksport, ME

18. Bully

Bully was my first English Mastiff. He was my world from the time he was six weeks old until the day he died at the tender age of seven. My children were teenagers and did not require much of my time, so it all went to Bully. He was always by my side and loved riding in my SUV. Everyone knew him at the local pet store and fast food drive-through windows. As much as he was a part of my life, he was also there for the children in my daycare. Every morning when I let the children go out to the playground, Bully was the first one through the door. He would run along the fence barking and letting everyone know not to mess with his kids; he was on patrol.

One day I heard a scream and turned to see the lawn man running to the gate with Bully in hot pursuit. He did not read the memo in my file that stated he must notify me before entering the backyard. After convincing him it was okay to reenter, Bully sat down and held out his paw; they shook and became best of friends.

Bully always went by my lead; if I accepted a person, he would also. If I was uncomfortable with a stranger, he could sense it and would put his large body in front of me and bark. They always got the message, loud and clear. On one occasion, a suspicious-looking gentleman followed me through a parking lot, and when I opened my van door, he saw Bully. "Cool dog," he said. "Can I pet him?"

"Sure," I said, as I was used to people wanting to touch this beautiful boy.

When he reached in, Bully growled and snapped at him. Wow, this had never happened before. I realized Bully sensed something in him that I couldn't, and that sometimes I had to trust him and follow his lead.

Lunch time in my daycare was Bully's favorite part of the day. He was not allowed in the dining area while the children ate, and he would wait patiently until the door opened and he was allowed to come in and consume all the leftovers. I called the kids inside for lunch one day expecting Bully to be the first one in but he stopped, sat on the stoop, and just stared at me. It was a beautiful day so I assumed he wanted to stay out for a while, and I closed the door. As I'm serving lunch, I realize that I'm missing a kid, and I rush outside. I look down at the playground and see my missing three-year-old on a swing with Bully, lying beside him. Needless to say, Bully got lots of hugs and treats and did not have to wait for leftovers.

My sweet Bully died at seven years old of bone cancer and I still miss him every day. He taught me about unconditional love and commitment.

He is the reason I will always have a Mastiff in my life.
Millie Spillers - Dacula, GA

19. TESS

Almost 20 years ago, we lost our Newfie to cancer. Of course we were lost without him. We have no kids, and we just adored our Buckwheat.

In the mean time, my route as a courier would take me by the animal shelter every day. I would stop in every chance I could get to love on the dogs and help fill the hole in my heart. Our neighbors had an all-breed book they loaned us, and that's where I read about the "Mas-teef." I had never seen one and had no clue how to pronounce "Mastiff," but I knew I was in love! I showed my husband the book and he agreed, but wisely said we need to do our homework and also see if we could even afford such a "rare" dog.

One day, while I was on my route, I saw a truck parked in front of a house that said "Wanna Be Run Training & Grooming." What possessed me to go knock on this stranger's door, I will never know, but I did. A very kind lady answered the door and said, "Hi, do you have a package for me?"

I said, "No. My dog recently died, and I saw your truck and was wondering what kind of dogs you work with?

She said "Bostons and Mastiffs."

I almost passed out! I told her about the book I was reading, and that my husband and I were trying to do our homework because we "thought" we really wanted this breed to be our next family member.

She took me in, introduced me to all her Mastiffs, and I was in love! I brought my husband back that night... We were hooked! The breeder, Lynda, had no pups and her bitch had just had a litter, so she had no breeding planned anytime soon. So we decided in the meantime to do more research, etc... and either wait, or maybe Lynda (the breeder) could recommend another breeder.

I continued to visit the shelter in our small town and then one day, there she was... a beautiful, young (guessing 10 months old) Mastiff bitch. It was love at first sight! She was so sweet. I asked one of the workers if she was up for adoption -- but got the runaround. I took my hubby back out there that night, even though they were closed, hoping we might be able to see her through the fencing; we could not.

We returned the next morning, as soon as they opened, so my husband could meet her. As soon as we walked to her kennel, she gave us a huge "WOOF!"

My husband said, "We have to get her!"

So again I asked a worker about her and got the brush-off. Finally one of the workers asked if we had talked to the manager, and I said, "No, but would love to!"

Apparently one of the workers was trying to get her out of there to breed her. She was in season. Once all of this came to light, the manager asked us a few questions regarding owning a large-breed dog; and next thing you know, she was ours and we were on our way to the vet to have her fixed.

We named her Tess after the movie *Guarding Tess*. She lived to be fourteen-and-a-half years old. She was all that a Mastiff should be. Over the years, she mentored many other rescue Mastiffs and a few of our pups. I truly believe God sent this angel to us to help heal our broken hearts, and me to Lynda so she could mentor me to be a great dog owner. She took me under her wing and we remain good friends to this day. We currently own three Mastiffs. Whether our dogs over the years were from rescue or our breeder, our Mastiffs have added so much love to our lives;

I wouldn't change a thing!
Carol Smith - Mesa, AZ

20. Dante

A Poem by Millie Spillers

Sweet boy Dante, life has not been fair;
afflicting you so young with a disease so rare.

I've watched you suffer for way too long;
to let it continue would just be wrong.

My heart is breaking for a life that cannot be;
for all the wondrous things you will never see.

I wish I could fix you, make it all go away;
and be able to share more spectacular days.

It breaks my heart to say goodbye;
I cannot bear to look in your eyes.

Mama loves you sweet baby;
sleep well, goodnight.

21. To My Bully Boy

A Poem by Millie Spillers

How do I say goodbye my friend?
My heart is so broken; will it ever mend?

I already miss caressing your fur;
so soft and warm, it makes my heart stir.

My tears have shed like rain today;
I pray dear God, take this pain away.

You taught me to notice the little things;
in all the wonder that nature brings.

To take a walk and not a run;
to bask in the warmth of a summer's sun.

You were always there at my beck and call;
never a moment did you stall.

There's emptiness beside me now;
I long for relief, some way, somehow.

I will so love the day when I see you again;
my baby, my love, my best friend.

Love, Mama.

22. Abby and Buddha

Everyone has a journey, one that changes your life. This journey is about my beautiful, sweet, innocent, loving, huge, monster dogs, Abby and Buddha. They are my loves, my heart and my life.

A few years back, I told everyone I was not a dog person and I wasn't... I loved them so long as they belonged to someone else... Then there was Nick, an English Mastiff, who has no idea of the impact he had on the rest of my life.

My husband and I went to Home Depot one Saturday. There was a rescue group at the Pet Smart next door displaying their homeless dogs. I went past as I always do, looking at them, feeling sorry at their plight. At the very end of the row of crates, there was one dog with a face so sad and compelling, I could not take my eyes off of him. He looked at me as if to say, "Please see me, please love me!"

He sat there calmly, head crooked to one side, eyes pleading to be loved. He was huge and beautiful, a dark apricot with black mask. His eyes were deep brown and penetrating, begging silently.

My husband joined me and I asked him to look at Nick, how sweet and beautiful he was. He backed away and said, "You are NOT getting a dog." I reluctantly backed away and eventually moved my eyes from him and we left.

Two weeks went by... but I could not get Nick out of my mind. So one day I called Pet Smart and asked for the name of the shelter who had been there that day. I called the shelter and asked if Nick had been adopted. They said he had an adoption pending. My heart was broken for me, but I was very happy for Nick. I do not know if the adoption went through, or if he is happy, if they kept or returned him; but I never saw Nick again with the rescue so I hope he is loved and well cared for. He remains in my heart to this day, and I think about him and his sweet face frequently.

After hearing of Nick's pending adoption, I started reading everything I could about English Mastiffs online. I was obsessed with this breed and felt an instant connection to them. I talked to my husband and updated him about the information I found. I called breeders and talked to them trying to get all the information I could. Everything I found out about them made me feel these were dogs we needed in our life. The only downside was their slobber, but that didn't bother me because the pro list was so much longer.

I wanted to rescue a Mastiff because there are few people who want these gentle giants. We contacted a rescue and scheduled for them to bring a dog named Max to us for a meet and greet. Prior to the meet and greet, my daughter had suggested watching Cesar Milan, the Dog Whisperer. So I watched every episode I could. The more I watched, the more confidence I gained in my ability to handle these monster dogs. So the day of the meet and greet was here; and Max emerged from the van, and he was gigantic. He was very excited and nervous because he was in a new and different environment. We took him for a walk, and using Cesar's methods, I was impressed at how well I was able to handle him, even though he was bigger than I am (at only 4'7").

Then we went into the house. We had a parakeet, Mango, at that time, and he immediately lunged for him, scaring him to death! The writing was on the wall. For the safety of Mango, we were going to have to get a puppy and raise it with Mango so he would be safe.

Max left and we were crushed. We decided to run to Petco, which was just around the corner from us. When we were about one mile from our house, there was a sign on a fence, "English Mastiff Puppies For Sale!" It was a sign. We did a U-turn and went back to the house with the sign. There were thirteen little Mastiff puppies, just four weeks old, without their mother. I was still pretty naive at the time and didn't realize this was way too young for puppies to be taken from their mom. We talked to the man with the dogs, then left to think about it. We got home and debated briefly, but knew we had to go back and get the cute little fawn female we had been holding. It was a cold, wet spring day; my husband went to get our little girl. He said the minute he walked in, the little fawn we had picked out jumped over all her siblings and ran to him. He brought this little three-pound pup to me, and I immediately took her to the sink and bathed her -- three times before she was clean. I blew her dry and held her in my arms for a long time to warm her because she was shaking.

That little girl, whom we named Abby, grew into a 130-pound beautiful, sweet, loving soul with a personality no one can resist. She is the love of our life. I know she would have died had we not taken her, because when we took her to the vet, he said she had worms and parasites in her tummy. She would have died within another week or two had we not taken her. I hope her siblings found homes because I am sure they were all in jeopardy.

We fell so in love with Abby and she seemed so lonely during the day while we were at work; so when she was approximately two, we started looking for another male Mastiff. I looked and looked all over the internet. One day I went to the online ads for the Dallas Morning News, and there was a picture of a beautiful six-month-old English Mastiff. He had the Nick-look on his face in the picture. I called my husband to the computer and said, "Look John, I think I found our dog."

We made an appointment to go see him at the breeder's home, and he came home with us. He walked right into the house, went straight to Abby's bed in front of the fireplace, grabbed one of her toys, and he was home. He fit right in as if he had always been with us. We named him Buddha; and he too is the sweetest, gentlest giant you could ever want. They are "yin and yang" being complete opposites, but they are alike in the sense they are filled with love and give it every minute unconditionally. They love each other devotedly and they both seem completely content.

Abby has always been a little hyper (still less than most dogs at her worst), which is unusual for a Mastiff and something attributed to her being weaned from her mom too soon. Abby is becoming less hyper as she ages, and is now more calm at three years old. During the summer, she expends her energy by swimming like a fish -- she loves the water and it is hard to get her out.

Buddha has always been completely calm. He, however, prefers to run through a sprinkler to swimming, and will only do one small circle in the pool, then gets out and gives you a look like, "I'm done now!"

Buddha prefers to sit back and watch everything, where Abby wants to do everything! Buddha is the cautious protector; Abby feels everyone was put on this earth to pet her, and they usually do!

If you are looking for a dog, a family member, a loyal and loving friend, you need to look past their size and slobber and see only their heart, which is larger than they are. A Mastiff, especially an English Mastiff, is the best dog in the world as far as I am concerned. I will tell you what someone told me:

"If you ever had one, you would never want any other dog."

And that is absolutely true, and you will want more than one. They are special and perfect -- at least for us. Now, because of Nick and my life with Abby and Buddha, I volunteer and help other dogs in need when and where I can. This journey is ever changing and evolving, and has given me the greatest love for dogs anyone could ever know. Nick was a gift, and I will love his sweet face forever!
Debbie Singer - Dallas, TX

23. Ruger

I had always had giant breed dogs my entire life, mostly Great Danes; so when I married my husband, it only made sense to have another one. Andrew didn't like or want Great Danes. A friend of ours had a Mastiff and I fell absolutely 100% in love with her! Five days later, I had my first English Mastiff and named him Ruger.

As any responsible pet owner of a giant breed dog, the most important thing is training, training, and training! I worked with him on my own for a while, and thought I was making pretty good progress with him. He walked politely on a leash, was potty-trained within a week, sat when I told him to, lay down when I told him too. The only problems I was having with him was: stay, come, and walking off a leash.

I decided to seek out a professional trainer for help. I did lots of research and found a man within miles of me who had awesome credentials in training and had several championships in the show ring. I talked to people that had taken their dogs there to be trained, and they all had wonderful results. How could I go wrong with this guy? Right? WRONG!

Before taking Ruger to this man, I went and checked out his facility and it was clean, bright and state of the art. It was great. The man convinced me that the best way to train Ruger was to leave him there for a week so that he would be able to work one-on-one with him more since he also lived on the site of the training facility. He told me that he loved Mastiffs and had always wanted one, so of course that sounded great to me that he wanted to be able to put in extra with my dog. I would find out a week later just how wrong this was.

The whole family went back a week later for OUR training session with Ruger so that he could show us what wonderful progress he had made with our dog. Everything went fine, and we were shown how to continue working with him to reinforce everything; and we were really impressed with the training he had received. Ruger was doing everything that I had tried to train him to do and just couldn't get him to do. It was awesome.

We took Ruger home and continued to work with him. I loved taking him out in public. People would come over to pet him (with permission from me of course) and he would sit politely and let them. Wow, this was amazing! Normally he would try to sniff them to death or paw at them. I couldn't believe how great my baby had turned out.

Shortly after bringing Ruger home, we decided to take him to Gladfest (a local street fair) where dogs were always welcome. This is where I got my first clue that something was wrong. My sister-in-law's father tried to pet him, and Ruger cowered away from his hand and then tried to bite him. I thought maybe it was just because we were in a large crowd, so I apologized and took Ruger home. Being the good dog mom that I am, I tried to reassure him the whole way to the truck that it was okay. Every time I tried to pet him he would cower from my hand. Ruger had never cowered a day in his life!

The next day, my then ten-year-old and two-year-old were downstairs playing tug of war with him while I was on the computer, when I watched Ruger bite my oldest on the leg. I was terrified that he would go after my youngest, so in his kennel he went. He tore a hole in my son's jeans, but didn't break the skin.

He had an appointment the next day at the vet for his yearly shots, so I decided to talk to him about Ruger's recent weird behavior. While sitting in the lobby, I could tell that he was a little stressed, so again I tried to reassure him -- more cowering, and then he tried to bite me! My vet ALWAYS runs late so we were in the lobby for about 30 minutes; and then my vet walked through the lobby, and as soon as Ruger saw him, HE WENT NUTS! He tried to go after him like he wanted to kill him. I finally got him into a room, and when the vet came in, again he went nuts and tried to bite the vet. Thank God I had a tight hold on his leash and could pull him away from the vet. Apparently that was a mistake, because he turned on me and jumped on me, and threw me into the wall and went after my face. As much as I hate to say it, the vet had to grab hold of him and throw him to the floor and straddle him just to subdue him.

We had to have another vet come in and take Ruger back to a kennel while we talked. Jeff and I spent an hour talking about everything; and while sitting there, I finally realized that he looked almost exactly like the dog trainer I had taken Ruger to. I commented offhand about that -- and he spouted off the name of the trainer. Right then I knew what he was going to tell me. I wasn't his first client that had taken their dog there and left it for a week for "extra training," then had this outcome. Apparently this particular trainer beats dogs into submission; and lots of people know it, but nobody can prove it.

Now I knew why my precious baby would cower from me or anyone when they tried to pet him. We just couldn't figure out why it happened two days AFTER he got home. I think maybe he was just happy to be out of there. My heart immediately sank to my feet, and I just busted out bawling! What had this bastard done to my dog? My vet and I decided it would be best if I left him there overnight so that he and the other vets could try to give him his shots; and so that my family and I could decide if I was going to bring a violent dog home.

Remember that I had a ten- and two-year-old at the time. If he went nuts again, he could have killed either one. Ruger was MY dog from the day I brought him home. He followed me everywhere and would prefer to be with me over anyone else. He slept on my side of the bed, he would lie outside of the bathroom while I was showering, and anywhere I went, he went. If he could turn on me like he did, I was terrified what he could do to one of my kids. My husband and I spent a long time that night trying to decide what to do. Many tears were shed that night, and we decided that it just wasn't safe to bring Ruger home. I also decided that I couldn't in good conscience rehome him in fear that he would try to attack someone else.

The next day, I went to the vet and told him my decision which he completely agreed with. He also informed me that none of the other vets or vet techs could go anywhere near his kennel without him trying to get through it to try to attack them. I went back to his kennel to try to get him out so that they could humanely put him to sleep, and once again, he tried to come after me. We had to trap him between the wall and the gate to give him just a little sedation to get him out (my heart was breaking and I was crying my eyes out). Once he was sedated enough, I sat down on the floor with him (yes I was taking a big risk) and gathered that huge baby on my lap while they put the IV in; I held him as he took his last breath. I stayed like that for what seemed like forever. I felt so guilty and kept telling myself that this was all my fault that I let this bastard beat my dog into submission and ruin him, even though I didn't know it was happening. I had Ruger cremated and he now sits in a beautiful urn on my dresser; that way I will ALWAYS have him with me. I have tried and tried (unsuccessfully) to figure out how to prove that this so-called trainer did this to my dog.

No other dog will ever replace my Ruger! I do have another Mastiff in my life now and he is a wonderful dog. He will never ever go to a professional trainer; he is trained at home between me and my other Mastiff friends, always using positive reinforcement! The moral to this story is check, double-check, and even triple-check your trainers. Get a list of their clients and talk to them. Now in the day of Facebook and other social media sites, put the name of the trainer out there and see what kind of response you get. Don't make the same mistake I did. Don't end up with a broken heart!
Tracie Balkey - Gladstone, MO

24. Ty

I was interested in the Mastiff breed but really didn't know anything about them, so decided to "foster" one to see how they would fit into my life. Don Crumb was to be my go-to guy. A bit of time had passed when I got a call from him telling me he had a Mastiff that needed help. So Don picked him up and we met halfway . This was the first time I actually met Don in person and he had this beautiful, fearful, fourteen-month-old, reversed apricot brindle boy with eyes the color of copper. His ears were completely absent of hair and he smelled horrid. He was sold by his breeder to a family who couldn't keep him; so they gave him back, and the breeder put him out in the back yard in a pen with his dominant father. Don noticed the father had the same bald, infectious-looking ears. His name was Hercules.

So off we went to start this new adventure together. I renamed him Ty, and after a month of oral antibiotics, finally the hair started to grow back on his ear. A good bath right when he came took care of much of the stench. He was my shadow, my boy right from the get go. I was his security. It took several months before he could remain in the presence of a man without peeing all over. It took six months before my husband could even pet him. He didn't have a mean or aggressive bone in his body, was just afraid. If I were in the shower, he was patiently waiting outside. If I were in my riding arena with my horses, he patiently waited outside. He was truly the most devoted friend I have ever had. His sole job, he thought, was to make sure I was safe and he kept a very close eye on me always. I was heartsick when I lost him to bone cancer at the age of 10. Tears of joy and sorrow as I write this.

You were right Don; I am also a mess writing this. There have been many Mastiffs that have come and gone to new homes on this property since Ty started it all (including Ty's litter sister and brother). Some always stay; others we have had good luck finding forever homes. Don told me at the very beginning that Mastiffs were addictive. He wasn't kidding. But we all have that one special child and without a doubt, Ty was my special boy.

To Ty: I miss you so very much. You gave me everything you had. I will forever hold you dear to my heart!
Pamela Bartlett - Williston, VT

25. Deniro

Deniro came to us via an abandonment. His owners moved and left him in the fenced backyard of the place they had been living in. Now there is no way they could have "forgotten" Deniro because he was five years old and he weighed in at 220 pounds. Forgetting a dog like Deniro -- impossible. Luckily, the people's landlord realized what had happened, and took him home and cared for him while she contacted rescue to find him a forever home. The women loved him and would have kept him in an instant if she didn't already have five Corgis in her household. She said he was so sweet and quiet, never bothered or was bothered by all the small dogs running around him, but seemed very displaced. After a series of phone calls and emails, we set up transport for Deniro to my house. However, my house was to be just a pit-stop for him on his way to his new foster/forever home. We had a family who had already adopted a Mastiff through rescue and really wanted a buddy for him. It was a fabulous home and everyone was thrilled. They were even coming to pick him up the same day he arrived at my house. This worked out perfectly because I happened to be leaving for a week vacation two days later.

Deniro arrived at my house looking very thin and downtrodden. We had set up a large yard for him to stay in while we waited for his new family to arrive. We didn't see much sense in introducing him to our other Mastiffs and possibly stressing him out even more. He seemed a bit confused but walked into the yard. Seeing his face and realizing how confusing it really must have been for him, I decided to go hang out with him for a bit to reassure him everything was going to be okay, and to get to know him a little bit to make sure he was going to be a good fit for the family. He was tentative at first, but after I sat down and continually talked to him, he came over to me and let me pet him. He was so sweet and eventually I felt him settle down a bit. I told him we had found him a great home and he was going to be so happy. After about 15 minutes, I headed out, and soon after, his new family came. We all went down to the yard, made introductions, and then eventually brought him up to their car. He never hesitated, got right into their car, and laid down. They were thrilled, he seemed content, and all was well.

Flying back from vacation, I called to check on Deniro from the Phoenix airport. I asked how everything was going and how he was fitting in with their other Mastiff and household. It was then they informed me Deniro was gone. I thought it was a joke, or that I had heard them wrong. I asked them to repeat what they had just said. They repeated he was gone. Midway through the week, he had jumped through the screen of a second floor window and vanished. They had been looking for him ever since with no luck. My heart sank. I had visited their house many times and knew exactly where they lived, in a mountainous, scarcely populated area. I also knew it was hunting season. All other plane rides have seemed short to me after that one home from Phoenix. We spent the next week scouring the mountains and hills around their home. We had fliers, offered rewards, contacted authorities, and local animal control agencies. Nothing. Deniro was gone. We were all devastated but refused to give up. The thought of possibly never finding him or knowing what happened to him haunted me every day he was gone.

Then one night, after him being gone for a week-and-a-half, we received a phone call from a woman who thought she might have found him. She and her friends had seen a giant, pathetic, thin-looking dog walking down one of the main roads in her small town. Mind you, this town was a whole mountain away from where Deniro's foster home had been. He wouldn't come to any of them, but they were able to corral him into a horse stall on her farm; and recognizing him from the fliers, they called us immediately. My feet never touched the ground on the way to my car. Adhering to all posted speed limits (yeah right), I made the hour-and-a-half drive to her house in fifty-three minutes. When I got there, they informed me he was in a bad state. Very thin, depressed, and would not eat or drink or even lift his head for anyone or anything. I took a deep breath, prayed it really was him, and opened the stall. It was him! I took a couple steps into the stall, crouched down, and said, "Hi Deniro." His head immediately came up, his tail started wagging, and he started pawing for me to pet him. They couldn't believe it. They all started crying; they were so happy to see him actually exhibit signs of happiness. I thanked them profusely, paid the reward, and drove Deniro back to the foster home. They thanked me and really just wanted to see him and make sure he was okay before he left to go to his forever home, at my house. It was a no-brainer for everyone, and they knew there would be more Mastiffs to rescue; and Deniro had made it pretty clear who he wanted to be with.

What a difference 15 minutes can make in a person's life. Deniro was my faithful companion for the remainder of his life, and I spoiled him rotten every day of it. He was an amazing friend, who rarely left my side. Even in his old age, when it was harder for him to get around, he always positioned himself in a place where he could see me. I feel honored he chose me to spend his life with. And as the old saying goes, it's not me who changed his life, it's Deniro who changed mine. I love you and miss you, my big Fathead.
Sarah Schreib - Williston, VT

26. Oodles

Dog shows can be so busy and stressful. Believe me, the one we were at was no different. I was busy grooming and cleaning up, when here comes a family asking about the dogs. At first I didn't bother to look up, just answered questions as I kept hurrying to do what I was doing. Then I heard the sweetest little voice. I turned to see the young girl sitting in a wheelchair. She spoke again in the weakest, softest voice, "Can I meet your Mastiffs please?" This little girl, very frail looking with oxygen in tow says, "I love dogs but we had to get rid of mine because I am sick."

At this point I had stopped everything I was doing, and started giving this little girl 100% of my attention. I started pulling Mastiffs out of the crate one at a time for her to pet, meet and love on. Her mother tells me how her daughter just adores dogs but since the cancer, and with all the treatments, they had to get rid of theirs. Several times the little girl has to pause because she is so weak. I have six Mastiffs with me, and she was so loving to each and every one of them. I get out the second-to-the-last Mastiff, a big boy named Oodles.

Oodles is a special Mastiff, as I knew he had a way with special needs children. Oodles sees the little girl and goes straight for her so gentle and easy, but makes it clear he was going to see her. He lays his massive head in her lap so gently. She wraps her arms around his big neck and just pushes her face onto the top of his head. She loves on him for a bit, and then I go to put Oodles in the crate so she could meet the next Mastiff. Oodles wanted no part of leaving her side. Finally, I get Oodles back into his crate so she could meet the last Mastiff. Oodles was so loud and clearly wanted out to be back with the little girl. So I get Oodles back out, and he goes straight for the little girl again.

She would cough, and you could see the concern in Oodles eyes. This very sick little girl is smiling and giggling as she whispers softly in Oodles ear. I will always wonder what she told him. They stayed for several hours so she could love on Oodles. He tried to climb up in her lap while she's still in her wheelchair; she just giggled. Clearly he would smush her, but he doesn't realize he is a 210-pound dog. He just wanted to be as close as possible to his new friend.

Oodles has a bad habit of nursing on things. I know it's strange, but he likes to suck on people's arms if he loves them. He got his giant head in her lap and started to nurse on her tiny arm, and he was ever so gentle about it. She just laughed and giggled and thought it was the funniest thing ever. Her parents sat down in my chairs beside her and were so-cherishing this special moment with their daughter. Her grandmother told me she has end stage cancer and doesn't have much time. She loves dogs so much that when they heard about the dog show, they had to bring her. Several times her mother looks at me and says, "We haven't seen her this happy in so long." This whole time Oodles is being this amazing gentle giant with her.

After several hours, her father says they have to go, as she needed her meds. As they go, the little girl is begging to stay and Oodles starts to walk off with them. He wanted to stay with his new special friend. Her dad caved; they stayed longer, and he just gave her the meds right there. Oodles watched so carefully. Oodles seemed to know this little girl needed him more than anything. Oodles was such a mush as the little girl just kept whispering secrets into his ear. You could tell she was getting so tired, but didn't want to leave Oodles. She kept saying, "He loves me so much," and he did. After many hours had gone by, they had to leave, and Oodles didn't want them to go. She gave Oodles one last kiss right on the lips. She looked right into his eyes and said, "I can go now because I met a dog angel, and I got my last wish to fall in love with a big dog."

Her parents asked if she could see Oodles again. I wrote down my contact info. I told them to call any time day or night, and we would have Oodles right there. As they walked away pushing her in the wheelchair, she ran her fingers through Oodles thick, Mastiff neck-fur, and got a bunch of hair in her hands. She looked up at me and said, "I want to keep his hair to remember him and his smell. His smell is something I never want to forget."

We never heard from her family. I fear the worst, but I know Oodles gave her one amazingly happy day. Oodles gave her and her family a special moment to share together that they, nor I, will ever forget. I know Oodles must think about his special friend sometimes too. This amazing gentle giant was there just for the dog show, and was able to touch the life of a special little girl and her family… which to me was more important than all the ribbons he had won that day.
Diane Green - Nashville, TN

27. Max and Jasmine

My brother has always been a fan of English Mastiffs. When he first brought one into his family, it was a rescue. Through him, we learned about Mastiffs and two organizations in our area, MUNY (Mastiffs Unlimited of New York) and FORM (Friends of Rescued Mastiffs).

In 2008, it had been a year since our first Bichon, Mandy, had passed away, and we decided that we could help the organization out by fostering. A need arose quickly, and we took in Max. When he first came to the house, we were a little skeptical about how our second Bichon, Rastus, would respond to him. Rastus was not very friendly with my brother's Mastiff, Gage, so we had our doubts. Max was very friendly and warm when he came into the house, and my gut said we were keeping him.

A week later, we adopted him. Traci had picked him up from the SPCA in Buffalo. The owner had dropped him off there and told them that he was not house-trained. He also told him that he could not keep him because he was locked up for up to fourteen hours a day. Since Max was five years old, if he was not rescued, it was likely that he would have been euthanized.

In the first several weeks of Max coming to live with us, he did not once go into the house. He had several health issues such as being underweight (145 pounds), having multiple ear infections -- and as time progressed -- we learned that he had a sensitive digestive system.

Max is such a loving dog that Rastus couldn't help but love him and accept him into our home. These two played just fine together. Max showed his true gentleness in being very careful not to step on Rastus; and when he does (accidently), he takes his punishment gracefully allowing Rastus to dominate him with confidence. Max has been a healthy 170-180 since we got him back to health. Max is currently going through some sort of allergic condition and requires two baths a week, a dose of antibiotics and antihistamine. He seems to be on the mend, and we are hopeful that his treatments will be successful.

In 2009, we heard about "Princess" in need of a new home from Don Crumb. Princess lived with breeders who decided to leave her in the dog pound one too many days to teach her a lesson for running away, because she had run away several times before. She and two or three of her pups had escaped; and when the owners went to pick them up, they were told they had to have the pups spayed and neutered, so they did not want them back. Our friend Don had actually gone to see her and left without her because she was so aggressive in the crate. The caretakers there had him come back, because they found out that she was not aggressive at all outside of the crate. Don went back and had her placed in a temporary foster home for a short time before we got word that she needed a home. Bill met the foster mom and spoke to her about the dog. As they were talking, she walked up to Bill and licked his hand. The foster mom said, "Did she just lick your hand?"

Bill said, "Yep."

She handed him her leash and said, "She is your dog." She was just telling him how Princess didn't like men. Princess, who was renamed Jasmine, came home with Bill.

Since we learned that Max has fear-aggression, which is more prevalent when he is with Bill or me, we enlisted the help of my brother and his wife to help us introduce Jasmine to Max. We did this in their front yard, then took them home in separate vehicles and let them free in our back yard to get to know each other. Jasmine ignored Max and was right at home from the day she stepped foot in the house and yard.

She has shown her escape capabilities by unlatching gates with great ease. The first time we went camping, someone did not latch the gate properly, so out she went to explore the neighborhood. I saw Max walking by the door of the camper, and realized they got out. I called Max who promptly came to me to be secured in the camper, and then I went to call Jasmine. I called her in a happy, friendly voice. She was a good distance away from me, but was not running… just sniffing around slowly going from one yard to the next on her little adventure. When I called to her, she came happily home; and as she did, I immediately praised her and took her into the camper. After all, she did nothing wrong. I was so happy that I could cry. She had no interest in running away at all. She has had plenty of opportunity to run away if she wanted to, but she is not anxious anymore. She feels safe, secure and at home.

Walking Jasmine, she always wanted to pull, so I decided I would let Max help me train her to walk nice. So I let Max walk on the outside, with his lead under Jasmine's chest. If Jasmine pulled ahead too much, Max would let her know it was unacceptable because she was pulling him too fast. Jasmine was always interested in whatever moved. It could be a bird, squirrel, person, vehicle, someone on a bike, anything. She would always pay more attention to what else was going on rather than walk nice. That meant she would ram into the side of your legs, take out your knee, or step on the backs of your heels. With the help of training tips from Susanne and Scott, she now walks nice with a loose lead, and she has calmed down considerably with her gate/crate/fence aggression. She still barks at things on the other side of the yard fence, but she stops when you call her; and if you call her and you tell her sit, she will without interest to what is on the other side of the fence. Jasmine has made so much progress in how calm and well-behaved she is; we could not be happier.

Bill and I are both consistent in our training with them and use the same commands. They are all on a regular schedule, and we send each other texts with what we call the "poop" report. Knowing that they are fed, exercised, medicated if needed, and that they had a healthy poop are very important to us. If someone did not take care of business -- that means that Bill will be right home to take care of them.

Max, Jasmine and Rastus are all walked regularly rain, snow or shine. They are all so well-behaved that I walk all three of them together with just me. If one is missing, my neighbors ask me where they are. They all play together well. They all enjoy camping and snuggling together in the comforts of their home. Even though they each came with their own issues and trying times, they give their love unconditionally in return for our efforts. Seeing them all snuggled together is priceless!
Dorinda Foos - Rochester, NY

28. Duncan

I lost my dog unexpectedly in April. She was a grand old gal and we miss her dearly, especially her best friend, our hound mix named Echo. I told my mom I thought we should get another dog to keep her company, as she missed Moria so. My mom said, "Get a mastiff."

I've always wanted a mastiff from the time I was a little girl. I said, "Okay," and we set about trying to find a mastiff puppy. My only stipulation was I wanted a brindle female.

I arrived home from work on a hot July day after working a long shift in a factory and my mom excitedly told me she had found a litter of mastiffs about an hour away that had two brindle females available. The owner said she would be home if we'd like to come and see them. I was tired but agreed we should go and see them.

When we got there, the puppies were playing in the kitchen and Betty, their breeder, said all of them were still available. I sat on the floor and was swarmed by playful puppies. They licked and bounced and rolled around; I think I must have been playing with them about an hour when I looked up and saw a brindle pup sitting directly across from me, just watching me play with his brothers and sisters. He never moved from his spot, just patiently waited. When all of the other puppies were done playing with me, they wandered off to nap. The little brindle fellow was still sitting there watching me. I looked at him and said, "Hi puppy. You can come see me too."

He stood up, walked over, climbed in my lap and lay down with a sigh. I rubbed his beautiful striped coat and he put his head up and looked me right in the eye. I knew he was saying, "You need to listen to me. I am your puppy; take me home with you." I held him for quite a while.

I said to my mom, "I know I wanted a girl, but that little guy is the sweetest thing."

She said, "If that's the one you want, then get him."

About half-an-hour later we were headed home with our new mastiff puppy on the front seat, soaking up the air conditioning in the car. I said to Mom, "He's such a dignified little guy. What do you think about Duncan as his name?" She declared it was perfect, so Duncan it was.

Duncan is like a brindle shadow. No matter where you go, he is there. Just like when he was a tiny puppy, he is always patiently waiting for you to notice him and invite him over for a scratch behind the ears or a big hug. He is always at the door when you get home with a full body wag to greet you. Even if all you do is walk to the mailbox, he gives you the same greeting.

It's like your a star and he is your most adoring fan. He makes you feel 10 feet tall. Every time you look his way, he is there just gazing at you with his heart in his eyes. No matter if you're just reading the newspaper or watching television, as long as he can lay his head in your lap, he is content. The only way to explain him is that he is my heart, and I am thankful every day that I listened to him when he whispered, "I am your puppy; take me home with you."
Bekka Walkos - Southington, OH

29. Chase

February of 2010, we adopted a two-year-old male Mastiff named Chase. He was a bit on the small side for a male, but we thought he was very handsome. He was loving, kind and wanted so very much to please us. He had one major problem though. Other than with the immediate family, and in some cases even some of them, he was extremely fear aggressive. I took him to my local animal shelter for training, and they said there was no hope for him at all and to consider putting him down.

I knew in my heart that wasn't necessary or right, so I searched for a trainer that would work with me and I found one. He said he felt that in his previous life, Chase had been pretty severely abused, hence the lack of socialization and severe aggression. Chase spent his first year of life basically locked in a garage until he went to a foster home where he was very well-treated. Our trainer also determined that Chase had to have been beaten because of his fear of certain objects and random unexplainable marks.

So Chase and I started with basic obedience and socialization in a class full of other dogs -- quite a challenge for him. By the time we were done, Chase was doing advanced obedience off-leash, and there was just the tiniest bit of the old fear-aggression left when he met a strange situation. It took 11 months, but we did it. Chase was so loving to my grandchildren and to my husband and myself, it is hard to describe. When I hurt my back, he came up to my bedroom and laid his head on my thighs as if he knew it would ease the pain for me. A dog couldn't have been more loved.

I would say to anyone considering a rescue to not be afraid to take a chance. He was my third Mastiff rescue but by far the most notable for a lot of reasons. I have never seen a dog so eager to please those he trusted.

Now comes the hard part. A week after we finished his advanced obedience class, Chase was diagnosed with advanced lymphoma. We were devastated. He seemed so healthy and active. We tried some holistic remedies and prayed and hoped, but it was not to be. We put Chase down on Valentine's Day 2011. He was with us one week shy of a year; but I wouldn't trade it for anything, and I am sure he is up there watching us and the two girl Mastiffs that came to live with us the week after he died.

Maryanne White - Webster, NY

30. Petra

Petra, an almost three-year-old fawn Mastiff, is responsible for saving my life and the life of my unborn child. I was having a difficult pregnancy and on bedrest after a short hospitalization due to placenta previa, a condition that causes hemorrhaging.

One Saturday morning, my husband had left for work and I was in bed still asleep. Petra had her own twinsize bed in our room, and always slept in the room with us. That particular morning after my husband had left the house, I heard Petra become a bit restless but assumed she was just repositioning herself on her bed, so I went back to sleep. I am not sure how much time passed, but she had come over to the bed and began nudging me with her cold nose, then tapping me with her big Mastiff paw, and then whimpering as if she was trying to tell me something.

These were all behaviors she had never displayed until that morning. I kept wondering, "What is her problem? Why is she so restless? Why is she bothering me?..." I was tired and still not quite awake. I knew she had been fed, had water, and had access to the outside. She was very persistent, and eventually I was fully awake. As I sat up, I realized that she was indeed trying to tell me something, as I discovered that I was again hemorrhaging. I was nearly eight months pregnant.

I called 911, and was transported to the ER and admitted to the hospital for several weeks until I gave birth via C-section to a perfect little baby boy! That was in May of 2005. From the minute I brought Wesley home from the hospital, Petra never left his side. She would put her head over his bassinet and peer in at him as if she was checking on him every so often. Then she would lie right next to his bassinet, almost tipping it over on occasion as she did the "Mastiff flop" to lay as close to the bassinet as possible. She was very protective of him.

We had to make the most difficult decision ever in June of 2010. Petra had severe arthritis and we could no longer manage her pain with medications. The day she left us to await for our arrival across that Rainbow Bridge was the saddest day of our lives.

My son, who was five years old at the time, displayed such wisdom stating, "There is no reason for us to be sad. Petra is in heaven now running around like a little puppy, and is no longer in pain." It was difficult to argue with that logic. If Petra would not have been there and had not awoken me that Saturday morning, I could have bled to death and lost my unborn son.

I believe it is because of the amazing instinct of our gentle giant and because she acted upon it, that her death has caused our family such heartbreak. Petra was true to her name and was definitely my "Rock" who I am grateful to have had in my life for those wonderful eight years. Every day that I look at my son, I know he is here because of her. She came into our lives for a purpose; she fulfilled her mission beautifully. We miss her dearly. Rest in peace my sweet Petra Claire!
Lisa Amos - Arapahoe, WY

31. Emma

Our journey with Mastiffs was not planned. In 1989, our beagle died unexpectedly. The kids were grown and we didn't think we'd have another pet. But a few weeks later, our oldest son appeared with a coworker's year-old Mastiff that needed a new home. Opal got out of his car, ran up the front steps with her head down, barreled into our home, and let us know immediately that she was not leaving. We were hooked on Mastiffs in short order. She stayed with us 11 years.

Next came Angus, a dog rescued from a NYC park where he had been tethered and abandoned. Unfortunately, he had not been fully screened and turned out to be food aggressive. With grandchildren in the picture, we were unable to keep him for fear of injuries to them. My husband Don had a very hard time letting go of him even so, and resolved not to have anymore pets.

But soon after, friends who had taken in two Mastiffs from one owner soon called and said "the boys" were too rambunctious and a danger to their smaller dog when rough-housing. Could we take six-year-old Charlie? We agreed to meet Charlie, and the rest is history. He brightened our lives and our home for another five years. He was the epitome of a great companion with a gentle soul.

At that point, we were well into our own retirement and really didn't think we'd take another dog. But, Don Crumb found us and told us about a dog whose name was just a number. She had been named for her birth order position which immediately told us she was probably considered to be nothing more than chattel. This dog had been returned to her breeder when the buyer failed to succeed in training her to become the mean guard dog he desired. It just wasn't in her to be that and her innate personality was stifled in the process. Once back at the kennel, she accidentally became impregnated by her own father and delivered a litter with some of the pups badly deformed. Her environment was not healthy in many respects and she suffered from neglect. She needed a loving home that would be patient with her and give her the attention and love she had never had. We were hooked again! And so, the dog with a number for a name became Emma, a name much more suited to her sweet, docile personality.

While Emma had no physical scars from her years of neglect, she definitely had signs of emotional trauma. The first few weeks with us, she chose to find the darkest corners of the house and curl up alone for hours on end. Little by little, she began to emerge and spend time in the same room with us. Eventually, she glued herself to a mat placed beside Don's easy-chair each evening. Meanwhile, he was walking her daily in the neighborhood working on her socialization. She would trail along behind him on her leash, never taking the lead. And when people were encountered, she was very reticent to let them touch her. Encountering other dogs terrified her and she would cower behind his knees. It took a full year of these daily exercises, and a huge effort on our parts, to provide a comfortable routine for her before her sweet personality began to emerge.

Now she stops automatically at the end of the driveway where a delightful preschooler lives. She watches and waits for Caroline to run out to see her. She loves her walks with her human dad and is on her feet ready to go as soon as she hears him click the hook of her leash. Oh she isn't exactly a speed demon. People often mistake her for an elderly dog because she moves so slowly. My husband counters their questions with a straight face saying, "We call her Flash. This is her high-speed mode." The inquirers just look mystified as Emma plods away from them.

Emma has been with us for three years now. We've seen her blossom into the most affectionate dog we've ever had. She still spends her evenings next to my husband's chair, usually upside-down and spread-eagle wanting constant belly scratches. Each evening Don gets down on the floor with her and they have a "chat" and a mush session before bed. She craves these routines and responds so sweetly to whatever we do for her and with her. While I'm her mom, there's no doubt whatsoever as to whose girl she is. She and my husband have created an ongoing admiration society that knows no bounds.

We don't know Emma's exact age. We think she's between six and seven now, as there are some gray hairs in her muzzle. She came to us afraid of tennis balls and soda cans, a fear that still controls her. She has never learned to play, so we don't see her get excited very often. But occasionally she breaks into a romp and shows us her desire to have some fun with us in the security of her own yard. We've loved all our Mastiffs equally over these past 20-some years, but Emma is indeed a special dog. She came to us with very special needs, and she has in turn given us a very special love. Her tail tells the story. It never stops. And lately she's begun to bestow morning kisses on both us while we're still in bed. We've created a love bug!

Emma will have several more years to love and be loved with us. Will there be another Mastiff after her? Don't ask!
Connie Halket - Holyoke, MA

32. Digby

Digby was the best friend anyone could ever have in this world. He was always a gentleman. As a puppy, he was so very serious, he gained the nickname "Little Man." As he grew, it became clear he was not going to be a show-off in the show ring. He had no urge to prance around; he went to shows just to meet people. He was a favorite of everyone, from little children to senior citizens.

His role with rescue dogs was so important. He constantly was used as a tester for rescue dogs, an example for puppies in puppy classes, and the "exhibit" Mastiff at club events. Foster dogs learned so much by his example. He was never mean. He was truly patient with new confused dogs, and he was able to calm the most nervous foster pup with just a look. No matter what I asked of him, he always complied. He was everything a Mastiff should be.

As a senior citizen, he has finally started to act silly. As an 8, 9, 10 and 11 year-old, he showed as a veteran in the Mastiffs Unlimited of NY Fun Match. Each time, the judge could not resist his upbeat personality and fun attitude. He retired at age 13 to allow "younger" veterans a chance to win! We realize that we were very lucky to have Digby. We were even luckier to have him for 14 years. He was such an enjoyable dog and truly was the perfect companion. Almost three years later, it is still hard to believe he is gone. Thinking about him will always bring a smile to my face.

Don Crumb - Penfield, NY

33. Ben

Ben was bought to be a companion for a man with some very challenging mental issues. When Ben turned seven years old, the owner's psychiatrist decided it would be better for the owner to give Ben away, rather than have him deal with an aging pet who would die.

Unfortunately, because of his owner's problems, Ben was never socialized and knew little of the world outside of his home. Fortunately, Laurie and Burleigh were willing to open their home and hearts to Ben. Their Mastiffs, Cagney and Thor, also welcomed Ben. The household cats, a pair of rescued littermates, never really warmed up to Ben; however, Ben never tired of being amazed by them!

Almost six year after Ben went to live with Laurie an Burleigh, I got the following update:

"Ben is now an incredible 12.5 years old and slowing down, but really doing very well. He still walks daily, (but just up and down the street), eats with gusto, and will pester us for milk in his bowl anytime he sees a glass on the table. He really sleeps about 20 hours a day now, but he OOZES joy, contentment, and -- believe it or not -- GOOFINESS for a couple of hours in the morning and evening before he passes out sleeping and snoring. He is a happy, easy-going dog, and has become more and more social over the time we have had him. Neighbors from all around the block always stop to visit him when they see him outside. He is SUCH a clown, he cracks us up at least once a day with his rumble-talking or the little "dance" routines he does... You have not laughed until you have seen a 170-pound Fuzzy Mastiff dancing like a Lhasa Apso. Sometimes he dances and rumbles at the same time.... It reminds you of Joe Piscopo in the Lethal Weapon movies."

Ben's happy ending is a reminder to rescuers that sometimes a miracle does happen, and a caring, qualified family will appear to take on a senior citizen with major issues. As we all know, the rescue folks do need these stories to keep them going and to give them encouragement. *Don Crumb - Penfield, NY*

34. Stella

Little baby Stella was brought to the shelter… At only 10-weeks-old, she had already seen the rough side of the dog world. She came from the "wrong side of the tracks."

Good friends who had been rescuer helpers were just getting over the loss of their girl, Marley. What better to heal the hole left by the loss of a beloved companion -- you guessed it -- than baby Stella? Stella caught on quickly that a Mastiff (even if she had questionable pedigree) deserved the better things in life. From swimming in an inground pool, to hanging out on real leather furniture, to sleeping on antique oriental rugs.

Shown is perhaps one or her baby pictures, showing she knows how to relax. Now she is all grown up, spending the summers in upstate New York and the winters in Florida -- what a life!
Don Crumb - Penfield, NY

35. Jacob

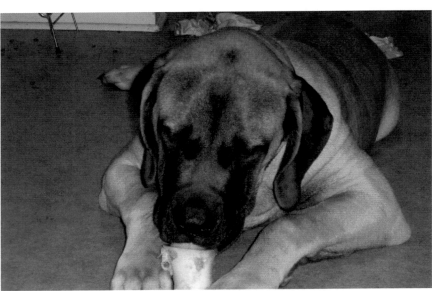

In a small rural town, the cops found the suspect they were pursuing had fled leaving 33 Mastiffs inside his disgusting garbage-filled house. The dogs were in horribly cramped quarters and some had never been outside. The local shelter could not handle the volume so everyone who could, helped out.

One day after the raid, Pearl ,an older Mastiff girl, gave birth to a litter of pups. They were the scrawniest pups ever. Each week, they grew but not as Mastiff puppies usually do. They were always undersized.

Jacob was the smallest. All three were full of personality and they each found great families. Jacob had a special job with his family. The family had two children. The oldest was a boy who was Jacob's buddy, and the youngest was a girl with some handicaps. She needed a puppy that respected boundaries and was always careful around her. Jacob filled the bill.

At about a year old, something strange happened to the littermates. They became giants -- each over 225 pounds and heights of around 35 inches at the shoulder. Despite his huge size, Jacob always remained calm and gentle with Sarah, his human sister. Unfortunately, Jacob did not have a long life; but in is short life, he made a real impact on Sarah. I am sure she will never forget him.
Don Crumb - Penfield, NY

36. Cleo

Cleo is full of it! Her antics cost her her first home. Her owners failed to train her or teach her any manners. The final straw came when Cleo stole the Thanksgiving Turkey. The rescue folks instantly liked Cleo and found her wildchild ways entertaining. Cleo went to her new home -- emptynesters who were not deterred by Cleo's reputation. Cleo still gets into trouble occasionally, but growing up and getting some quality parenting has made her much better behaved.
Don Crumb - Penfield, NY

37. Cloey

I received a call that an elderly couple had a nine-month-old Mastiff puppy they could not control. I immediately went to meet Cloey. She was a skinny brindle girl who could melt your heart; however, she had another side. She was produced by a "breeder" who bred two Mastiffs with very bad temperaments. Neither parent had AKC papers or any health testing. In addition to the problem of poor genetics, Cloey had no puppy socialization. The combination made her very fearful of new people and very toy aggressive toward other dogs.

Many potential adopters were interested in Cloey because of her age. (It is amazing how quickly word travels when there is a puppy in rescue.) No one was suitable to help Cloey reach a higher level of behavior, until the Kimpel family came along.

The parents, Dave and Elaine, seemed perfect, but I was hesitant because they had teenagers. Once I met Chris and Jena and saw them interact with Cloey, I knew they were amazing young adults. Their gentle and patient attitudes could be an inspiration for many older dog owners. All four family members worked hard to make a home for Cloey. Her challenging behavior has never detoured them and she has made amazing progress.

A fifth family member, a senior citizen St. Bernard-mix named Penelope, also helped Cloey adjust. Penelope has since passed, but I am sure there is a special place for her in heaven for putting up with all of

Cloey's oddities. Cloey is a character who will always entertain those who know her. From her frog hunting at the family pond, to dissecting stuffed toys, to sledding Cloey-style, to mouthing off at strangers -- life with Cloey is never boring!
Don Crumb - Penfield, NY

38. Bear and Zyta

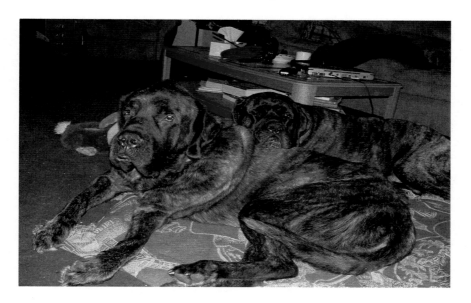

Bear was owned by a young couple who were in the process of getting a divorce. The wife could not take Bear with her, and because of her husband's temper, Bear was not safe with him. Despite his young age, his hips were a mess. He met Mark, Kathy, and Amanda and they didn't mind at all about his special needs. He immediately fell for them and their lab, Buddy. Through some modifications, they were able to make their RV "Bear-accessible." The five of them did camping and traveling, and Bear learned how to be properly spoiled!

Then a couple of years later, I got a call from a girl in college regarding her pet Zyta. The girl's mother had decided she was tired of dog ownership, and Zyta had to go. The girl was devastated. She loved Zyta and had been putting so much effort into being sure she was a perfectly trained Mastiff. At a picnic, Mark and Kathy met Zyta; once again, they fell head over heels for another brindle. At the next visit, Zyta won over Amanda, and then convinced Buddy and Bear that she was the sister they needed.

Now they are all living as one big happy family! It was nice to be able to tell the upset prior owner that Zyta had hit the jackpot and was living the life every Mastiff deserved.
Don Crumb - Penfield, NY

39. Hattie

Hattie was found by our city police locked in the second floor of an abandoned house. She had recently had a litter of pit-mix puppies, and then was left to die. Luckily, our city shelter knows that we are actively involved in Mastiff Rescue. She was about a year old. She weighed 64 pounds, had several wounds and sores on her legs; she had lost considerable muscle tone in her front legs. (When she walked her pastern was almost on the ground.) She had scars on her face and around her eyes (the vet believes it could be a result of dog fighting), and she was unable to digest food.

Our vet questioned our decision to try to nurse her back to health -- he warned us that it could be a lengthy recovery process with no guarantees that she would ever be healthy or emotionally stable. Carol and I both agreed that although her body seemed so weak and frail, her eyes were that of a dog that was full of life. We felt that we owed her the opportunity to recover. Carol used T-Touch on Hattie, she obsessed about Hattie's diet, and cuddled her whenever possible.

Despite her dog-fighting background, Hattie never showed any aggression to our other two Mastiffs; instead, she seemed to model their behaviors as much as possible. Her over-protectiveness of not only Carol and I, but of our other dogs, showed she was probably not adoptable through the rescue program; however, this was a moot point.

All members of our household, canine and human were so quickly bonded to her; we could never let her leave. Throughout her life, Hattie continued to learn how to control her mistrust of strangers and situations. She would look to us for cues and learned to put herself in timeout. (She would head upstairs to our bedroom and wait until she felt calm enough to return and visit with guests.) Her house manners were perfect and she became a valued companion.
Don Crumb - Penfield, NY

40. Hestia

09/06/2010

Hestia was found in Sidney, Ohio, as a stray guarding a garbage can. When animal control found her, she was in very bad shape. She was very underweight, the pads on her feet were raw and bloody, and she had a great deal of hair missing on her hindquarters. She had obviously given birth to too many litters of puppies.

Once she arrived at the shelter, they wanted her to be euthanized for many reasons: the bad shape she was in, she was a "big black dog" that they figured no one would want to adopt, and she had some aggression issues. Those issues were only when something caused her pain and she was food aggressive due to being starved. One of the nice animal control officers seen something in her worth saving, so he took her out of the shelter and brought her home to his house and family where they got her the vet care she needed, got her spayed, and fed her regular healthy meals. She soon lost her food aggression once she realized that she was no longer going to have to fend for herself.

They became very attached to her and kept her for almost a year, working with her and giving her the love she so desperately needed. They knew they could not keep her; they had a Neapolitan Mastiff and another dog, and financially it was just too hard for them. That is when they contacted me, a regional coordinator for another Mastiff rescue.

So I contacted the rescue I was with at the time and was told she was too old, that no one would want to adopt her. Her age was guessed at approximately five to six years old. So, me loving the seniors like I do, and the fact that my other two Mastiff girls had passed away in the past year, I decided to adopt her myself. Hestia's foster dad met us in northern Kentucky in May of 2010. She came to us with a bad ear infection and bad teeth; four of them have since been removed, so now she really is a tooth-missing hillbilly girl. She also suffers from some arthritis, but if we can keep her from jumping and running around too much, she does fine. We were told she did not walk well on a leash and hated going to the vet. She still hates the vet, but with a little work, she is a joy to walk on a leash.

The first two weeks she was here, she would sit by the front door and cry; and if she was outdoors, she would sit by the gate out to the driveway and cry. She missed her foster family so much, it just broke my heart to watch her be so distressed. It was probably the first time in her life she knew what it was to be loved and taken care of. Eventually she got used to us and started warming up; she really prefers men to women and is my husband, Ken's, best buddy.

We noticed immediately that Hess, as we call her, was very sensitive to her environment and daily life. Everyone who meets her says she has the most serious look on her face, but I prefer to call it a concerned, caring look. She knows when I am having a bad day; she will be extra affectionate and loving to me even though I still have to ask for a kiss, which she gives to Ken regularly. She never forgets anything; once she has learned a new word, it's ingrained in her forever. I have learned to spell out words, like "ride" for example, so she does not hurt herself jumping around in excitement. Last summer we had an opportunity to get together with her foster family from Ohio, and she remembered them immediately. It was interesting watching her go back and forth between them and us as if she was trying to show us all attention, not wanting to hurt anyone's feelings.

In February this year, one of our other rescued dogs, Murray, who had just turned 10 years old, was diagnosed with cancer and a degenerative spinal cord issue. Hess seemed to know something was wrong with Murray before anyone else knew. A couple of months prior to his diagnosis, she had been sticking by his side much more than she had previously. She would go over to him and lay down beside him, even though he would always get up and move somewhere else. Murray was not a social dog when it came to other dogs; he tolerated them, but pretty much ignored them. She was very persistent, and at the time, I just thought she was trying to bond with him.

But then I noticed that even when they were outdoors, she seemed to follow him all over the yard, which she had not done before. After Murray was diagnosed and had surgery to remove the cancer, he did not recover. His spinal cord issue grew worse by the day until he could no longer walk unassisted and had lost all bladder and bowel control. Hess stayed by his side, helping me to keep him clean, like he was a newborn puppy.

Then one morning as we were lying by Murray, he let out the most awful sound I had ever heard a dog make before... Hess got up and started pawing at me, and kept going back and forth to the door, then back to me. I asked if she had to go out, but every time I opened the door for her, she would back away and go back to Murray. Murray looked really bad that morning, and I knew the day had come to let him go. As we lay there with him, I asked Hess if it was time to let Murray cross over to the Rainbow Bridge. And yes, I know she did not know what those words meant, but she started the pawing-the-door thing again, then came over and gave me a kiss and started licking on Murray. I think she was trying to tell me that our dear Mr. Murray had had enough and just wanted to go to sleep.

It amazes me how some animals can be so in tune to what is going on around them. I am positive they have a sixth sense, or something equivalent. She has even taken on some of Murray's traits, things she never did before.

The first few years of Hestia's life were nothing more than her being used as a breeding machine. She knew nothing but pain and a life without love. She has a hematoma in one ear due to an untreated ear infection, something her previous owners felt that spending money on for vet care was not necessary. She has come a long way from that starved, scared girl that animal control picked up. She is sweet, very affectionate, smart as a whip, and has a mystical soul. She can now spend the rest of her life being spoiled and loved. We adopted another Mastiff, Lucy, last summer and they are best buds, always together, even sharing the same bone to chew on at the same time.
Dusty Kenly - Waco, KY

41. Monty and Chloe

There were days when I couldn't get out of bed, wondering if my life would ever be the same. I knew that, based on my diagnosis, I would be unable to work and that I would be spending many days and months in bed recovering, trying to get strong enough for surgery. I was scared, felt alone and unable to understand how, just a month before, everything seemed to be fine.

The love of an English Mastiff is like no other. The devotion is unmatched. The way they understand what you are saying, feeling and needing. The slobber! If you love an English Mastiff, you love their slobber too. The way they look at you with such love and give you a big smile. They just know. The way they want to nuzzle their heads up against you and cuddle -- and they LOVE to cuddle. There is no other love like English Mastiff love. Although I knew it prior to my illness, I did not realize how much their love helped to save my life. They know that they have been given a special gift.

I am blessed because I have two wonderful and loving English Mastiffs: a beautiful brindle male named Montgomery Baskerville, a.k.a. Monty, and a pretty female named Chloe Elizabeth. The days I spent in bed recovering from a life-changing diagnosis were only made bearable by the love of my English Mastiffs. They would spend endless hours up on the bed with me, comforting me and cuddling with me. They knew I was ill and they knew I needed them.

It took me six months at home on disability, a major surgery and recuperation before I was allowed and was able to return to work. During those months, there were very dark and scary days, but my English Mastiffs knew I needed them; and when I needed someone to talk to, they were there. Many days I would get up and bawl my eyes out and I just couldn't stop. They cared. When I needed someone to comfort me while I cried, they were there. When I needed to feel loved because my appearance was rapidly changing and I couldn't stop it, they were there. When I needed someone to talk to, they were there. Most importantly, my English Mastiffs were my best friends during one of the darkest times in my life and never left my side. They made my days brighter, bearable; they comforted me and shared their unconditional love.

Without the love, devotion and loyalty of my beloved Monty and Chloe, I do not know how I would have survived those long and scary months. Monty would jump up on the bed and come right up to my face and give me big kisses, and then nuzzle his head into my neck and chest while I kissed on him and rubbed his chest. He would lie as close as possible to me always making sure he was touching me with his paw or laying his head on me. Chloe would jump up on the bed doing her best to move Monty out of the way so she could get close and cuddle. She has been a little insecure since she was a puppy, but she showed me that she was a confident guard dog, making sure I was well-protected. No matter what room of the house I went to, they followed, making sure I was okay. They were my best friends and confidants and I will be forever grateful for their love and support.

Yes, there is nothing like the love of an English Mastiff -- they just know.
Patti Miller - Phoenix, AZ

42. Georgia-Girl and Figgie-Fig

I fully believe that your first Mastiff should come with a warning. They are not like any other breed. A Mastiff demands to be in your heart and is emotionally tied to the whole family. They are born with the ability to establish themselves there. They have a sad, guilty "how could you" look that should win each one of them an Oscar.

I am honored every day to read and live the funniest story ever told through my Mastiffs' eyes and antics. I promise that each one of the stories doesn't compare to the real thing. Georgia-Girl was our very first English Mastiff. No, she didn't come with a warning. She knew, even as a puppy, that she had the upper hand. Our whole neighborhood, neighbors, our town, and us thought she was the cutest thing on earth. I have come to realize the South is just learning the masterpiece the Mastiff is. She became a diva very quickly and decided that this was the life!

I learned very quickly that I was going to have to get onto her while laughing in a pillow. I'm still waiting for me to show up on Youtube as the crazy lady trying to get her Mastiff puppy in. Georgia-Girl loved outside, for our neighbor adored her. He had special treats for her and always saw things her way. I don't blame her for deciding that being outside was the greatest, but Mom wanted her inside. Of course, everything seemed a game to her, for who would ever think she could do anything wrong? I would stand at the back door and yell for her to come in. She would always give me that look like, "time to play." I would walk a few inches from her and then she would dash to the other side. I would go to the other side, and then she would dash to the other side. I can only take so much; so by the time we had done this for a while, I am done. I always come to the only thing that comes to mind… I know there is a military school for dogs! Of course, she tilts her head like, "Please." I finally give up with her following me in the house thinking that she is ready for her treat. She was a puppy then and obeys now, but I am still convinced that I still see that look of play flash in her eyes.

Our second English Mastiff is our Figgie-Fig and she is our adopted baby. We co-own her with her other wonderful mommy. Georgia-Girl has always been an English Mastiff with a bee in her bonnet. She does things differently than most Mastiffs, but we wouldn't have her any other way. Figgie-Fig is the true character of an English Mastiff with manners. I was in the hope that Figgie-Fig would teach Georgia-Girl some of her good manners. She has taught her some, but Georgia-Girl has taught her a few of her own. It is like watching my own Lucille Ball Show.

My girls could not be more opposite, but they love each other deeply. Figgie-Fig still looks guilty when Georgia-Girl has done something wrong. Georgia-Girl still has the look of, "It was worth every second!" English Mastiffs don't usually flip in the air, and Fig totally agrees with this at 160 pounds. She runs like a dancing bear, but her idea of a good time is her soft bed. Georgia-Girl loves to dance, flip and jump in the air. I have to tell you that she has longer legs and only weighs 110 pounds. I am on Figgie-Fig's side on this one. They both like to play the sneak game and rough-house.

I love to watch them outside when they are really playing. It is usually during this time that Georgia-Girl loses her mind and jumps over Figgie-Fig from nose to tail. It is at this time that Figgie-Fig rolls her eyes (promise) and gives me the look of, "She is a disgrace to the Mastiff race!" She sits by me and ignores her sister totally. Her tolerance of Georgia-Girl's antics has a limit. Georgia-Girl loves to show off to anyone, but she is learning with her sister that it only goes so far. My two girls have such a bark, that my mailman has never been seen by anyone. We get our mail, but it has to be a world record on delivery time.

I do believe my girls would protect my husband, myself and my four kids (twins). I don't believe they go looking for danger. This is why I call my girls "chicken butts." I do have a few stories that will back up my claim. It first came to my attention when Georgia-Girl went out with my kids to the pond. I have pictures that in no way is she acting like there are ducks in front of her. It is her picture of, "I'm not afraid of any ducks for I do not see any ducks! I am protecting them from the alligator." This was the beginning of acting bad-to-the-bone until we had to act upon it.

Georgia-Girl also flies out the door to have ladies time outside. She will try to chase the same squirrels away from her fence. The male squirrel finally stood up to her. She turned to me with that look like, "What do I do now?" Figgie-Fig doesn't waste her time, for she goes out for two seconds and back to the heat or cold air. She suffers for no one. She will though, warm my feet, always keep me on my nap schedule, watch my kids, and is very much like a momma hen. Georgia-Girl is more like the baby sister who is always up to something. She hides Figgie-Fig's baby puppy toy. She will hide any toys and totally forget where she put them. She is really too smart for her own good.

I use to be known for having three babies under the age of two with a triplet stroller. I can honestly say that my English Mastiffs get the same attention. They are truly the gentle giants with a personality just as big.

The first of November 2011, I was getting really sick. I had one seizure about a year before, but they never found a cause. I did get better, and after a year, got my licenses back.

My Mastiffs love to sleep especially my Figgie-Fig. I started feeling really weird again. It was 36 hours before the incident. Figgie-Fig and Georgia-Girl hovered over me to the point it was upsetting. They wouldn't let me out of my bed. I finally got the hint and went to MUSC Hospital. I couldn't see my regular doctor, so I went to the clinic. I was coming in telling them my Mastiffs were acting like I was about to have another seizure. They looked at me like I might be a little nuts. I went home, and at 2 AM, woke my husband up to take me to a local ER.

They told me again, I was dehydrated and having an anxiety attack. I told them again about my English Mastiffs. There must be something really wrong with me for my English Mastiffs to be missing their sleep time. I walked to the waiting room after they released me. Of course, I went into a full seizure waiting for my husband. I don't remember anything until I woke up on the neurology floor. I am still in testing at MUSC, on major medicine, losing my hair and can't drive again. My big

babies know how to take care of their mommy. They are my four-legged kids, by my side always, knowing when I need sloppy kisses, and knowing when I need to laugh -- and most of all -- my heroes!
Tania Palmer - Summerville, SC

43. Laird Duncan

All of my natural life (that's a very long time), I had certain rules established for dogs. Some of these rules were my own rules; most were handed down by my mother who was definitely not a dog lover.

Dogs were not ever to be fed from the table. This was the number one rule, and both family and dog adhered to the rule.

Second rule was no dog was allowed on the furniture. Dogs had their own bed or a crate. That was it, period, end of story. No dogs on the furniture.

Probably the paramount third rule was that no dog ever could sleep in a human's bed. Dogs had their own bed and humans didn't sleep in it, so no dog was allowed on a human's bed, whether it had someone in it or not.

Almost seven years ago, my daughter, Becky, brought home an English Mastiff puppy whom she promptly named Laird Duncan Largepaw.

Duncan looked into my eyes, and my rule book went out the window. When a Mastiff looks into your eyes, they see your soul.

I would hold him on my lap while sitting on the couch watching TV. At one point, Becky chided me saying, "Mom, you always said 'no dogs on the furniture.'"

I told her that he wasn't on the furniture, as I was holding him on my lap.

She replied, "Mom, he weighs 80 pounds and the only part of him that's on your lap is his head."

Next rule was no feeding from the table. This rule got changed so much that if I was eating the last morsel and Duncan looked at me, I would remove the piece from my mouth and hand it to him. It always made me feel like a mother bird when I would give him that last bit of food. I think I would have been alright with this rule if he had worn a blindfold.

The bed part is also my fault as he would take that great big head and put it on the side of the bed and look at me with those eyes, and I would get out of bed and boost him into the bed. That was fine when he was a puppy, but at 160 pounds, it takes two people to toss him onto the bed now.

The amazing aspect of all the perks Duncan has managed to obtain from me, is that he doesn't demand anything; I just want to do all this for him. The other issue is that he has found a genetic flaw in my family because Becky treats him the same way. He makes us want to do these things for him, and we tell him we believe he's perfect.
Madeline Walkos - Chagrin Falls, OH

44. Shambeau

In 1976, my friend Shirley Lyons asked if I would evaluate a Mastiff she wanted to rescue from a family threatening to shoot him. Apparently everyone was afraid of this "dog from hell." She traveled from upstate West Virginia and with the help of several men armed with clubs, she loaded the beast into a wooden crate and returned to Huntington. Later that day, she backed her truck to the rear of my training center. "What's his name?" I asked.

"Shambeau," she said, "and he's big."

My training center is a clear span building, 50 feet by 60 feet. I stood in the center and told Shirley to turn him loose. He bursts into the room like a freed Mustang... snorting and throwing his head as he pranced in a large circle. He was 200 pounds of pure muscle. As he strutted he kept his head high, looking for a means of escape.

Five minutes later I stopped watching him, sat in the chair, lightly whistled and called to him. At the time, he was behind me watching me closely, according to Shirley. "C'mere boy," I said softly, but firmly called. He would either come without a second command, or he would ignore me with no intention of changing his mind. This was a dog that made decisions of trust immediately.

Five seconds later he slid under my arm and sat at my side while looking straight ahead, not necessarily aloof, but rather confident.

"What do you think?" called Shirley.

I turned to him and stroked his broad head. "I think he's the best representation of the breed I've ever seen," I told her.

Shambeau and I became inseparable friends. He won Best of Breed at the 1977 Mastiff Club of America Specialty Show and Best of Breed at the 1977 Westminster Kennel Club Show in Madison Square Garden. Champion Greenbrier's Shambeau was retired to stud service the following year. This was his preference, not mine, but he had had his fill of city lights, preferring instead long afternoon naps in Shirley's living room.

Shirley had rescued this wonderful beast from those who would have taken his life. How fitting that he would stay by her side until he died six years later.

He was one of the great dogs of my life, rescued from the hills and crowned at Westminster.
John Preston Smith - Huntington, WV

45. Izzy

Many years ago, my boyfriend and I had an English Mastiff named Snoodle Bear. I loved her dearly, and when she died, I vowed that one day I would own another one just like her.

Years later, I became a wife and mother and my family knew the story of my Snoodle Bear. My husband always said he would get me another Mastiff once we could afford it.

One night while browsing on Craigslist, I found a litter of Mastiff puppies for sale. They were priced very low, so I assumed it was a backyard breeder and the pups would come with a lot of problems. My husband told me it wouldn't hurt to just go look at them.

The next day my kids and I went to see these one-week-old puppies. The mama Mastiff was skin and bones, and I don't know how she birthed these babies just one week earlier.

I knew if I took a pup I would be taking home a lot of issues down the road, but what if I didn't? I felt I had to try and save one of these tiny babies.

I let my children pick out their favorite one, and it was a little girl they named Izzy Belle.

The next week when we returned for a visit, I was told that the mother dog could no longer feed them and the owner was giving them puppy chow soaked in warm water.

When the puppies turned five-and-a-half weeks old, the owner called me and asked if I would go ahead and take Izzy. She said the pups were not dependent on their mom, so it wouldn't hurt. I think it was to make things easy for herself. I knew that was too young for a puppy to be taken from their mother, but I feared that she would not be cared for if I left her.

When my friend and I arrived to get Izzy, the owners were all smiles and bragging that they had just given her a bath -- but Izzy wreaked of something. I couldn't put my finger on it, but she flat-out stunk, and it was the same smell that was in the owner's yard and home.

I brought her home and she joined my pack, Lola and Reese. She was very sweet, but not playful like a puppy should be. I took her to the vet the next day and found out she had Coccidia, hookworm and roundworms. I was not alarmed since I grew up in a family that raised Boston Terriers and knew that puppies do get these things. Then the vet told me if I had waited another day to bring her in, she would have died. I understood this as soon as I cleaned up her first poop. A mound of worms larger than my fist came out of her tiny body.

I called the breeder to inform them that the other puppies should be treated for worms, and was informed that all her puppies were just fine. I will always wonder how many of Izzy's brothers and sisters survived that horrible place.

We watched our Izzy make a full recovery and start growing like a weed. But still this day she is on the small side for her breed.

She loves playing ball and going up into the kids' playhouse and sliding down. She is smart, funny and has an amazing personality.

She recently walked in her first parade and remained calm among the crowd and all the children rushing to pet her. She was so loving that we think she will make a good therapy dog. My family is blessed to have this sweet girl in our life. Izzy's first birthday was on April 12, 2012.
Miranda Miller - Indian Trail, NC

46. Henry Sue

This is Henry Sue
explaining his terrible, horrible, no good, very bad day:

I've had a really bad day. When Daddy went to take a shower, he told me to be good, but he didn't put me in my pen. Well I got bored real quick, so I headed to the kitchen. I found this yummy-smelling plastic jug and I had to check it out. How could I resist; it smelled like French fries, fish, bacon and sausage all rolled together. Once I sunk my teeth into that jug, a delicious oil came spilling out. After chewing for a bit, I noticed there was a large puddle of this delicacy on the floor. I had to roll in it and cover myself with it's aroma. After getting all slicked up, I ran excitedly all through the house.

Daddy got out of the shower and immediately saw my footprints. He yelled at me to stop walking through Gracie's water bowl. As he started wiping up my mess, he got a funny look on his face, he stood up, and followed my prints all the way to the jug on the kitchen floor.

Then he really yelled, "Oh Henry Sue, what have you done?" My yummy liquid had soaked into the rug and the bottom of a box of papers.

I still had some puddled around the recycling bins. Daddy started muttering things in a funny language, then he cleaned me up and put me in my pen. I took a nap.

Suddenly I woke up with a sharp pain in my belly. I had to GO, I had to GO now! Oh no, Mom and Dad aren't home; I gotta HOLD it. Nope can't do it, gotta poop now. I jumped out of my pen, ran into the front room, and let loose on the tile floor. Boy did it stink, but I felt more coming so I ran to the oriental rug and dumped there too. I just kept pooping all through the house and then my tummy felt all better.

Pretty soon Daddy came home and his eyebrows went way up high. He said, "Henry Sue, how did you get out of your pen without unlatching it?" Then he started sniffing around until he found all my mounds of poop. Poor Daddy got out the cleaning supplies and was busy again.

When Mommy got home, I felt much better. She said that I smelled like a diner, and why was my fur and collar all greasy? She gave me a nice bath and a new collar; I love you Mommy. And Daddy, I hope tomorrow will be a better day.

By the way, I am a boy not a girl. You'll have to ask my mom about why she named me Sue.
Cheryl Winters-Heard - Mobile, AL

47. Annabelle

My great beauty, my queen, my companion and best friend passed away two days ago at the age of eleven.

By God's grace, I received Sara, renamed Annabelle, five years ago in October. MCOA had rescued her from a puppy mill in Missouri. With the help of several families, Anna reached me outside a restaurant in southern Wyoming. The first time I saw her, she was huddling in some bushes, frightened but regal. On the way to her forever home, I comforted her the best I could for the two-hour drive. Anna had never been outside, seen a window, traveled in a car, sniffed grass, lay upon a bed/couch, or able to potty outside her cage. She weighed 115 pounds which was mostly weight she had put on while in foster care.

It was a very long, difficult journey for both of us as she gradually came out of her shell. However she was able to enjoy traveling in the car, looking out the window and going to the park. She would gaze out the hatchback window happily from her safe spot. She grew to love the outdoors and became more of a dog as time went on. A special memory I have of my darling is seeing her give a warning bark at some unknown menace from the safety of the kitchen door. She would utter a gentle "woof woof" and then come to me with a slight ruff-up for a rewarding pat. That was so wonderful to me and to her.

Her end was quick. I think she experienced a stroke in the night and was unable to use her back legs or bark for help. I made her a throne of soft quilts and waited for the vet to come. While we waited, I brushed her coat, sang to her and spoke lovingly to her constantly. She became more at ease, and by the time the vet came, I think she was ready to go.

I celebrate her life and know she gave me a thousand percent more than I gave her. She is being cremated, as all my babies are, and will be back home next week.

She loved children; meeting new people; barking at the fence; going to the park; eating chicken, carrots and broccoli; having her belly scratched; being with me and my family; cuddling on the bed; and lounging on her pillow. She is survived by another MCOA rescue, Pete a Bull Mastiff.

God Bless you MCOA for giving me this wonderful time with my beautiful girl.
Linda Hartman

48. Harmony

I was a new admirer of English Mastiffs, had never seen one up close but was captivated by their pictures. Their size, gentle expression and easygoing ways made them sound like a perfect fit for my family. We could not afford a puppy so decided to check out rescues. Through Google we found a Mastiff rescue nearby and contacted them. They matched us up with Harmony, a 160 pound lovebug. Looking back, I think we probably made her first day too stressful. We had visitors that day with small kids and took her on a very long walk. She remained calm, came through with flying colors and we knew it was a match made in heaven. She followed me around for a couple of days but stayed away from my husband. We think she had never been around men before. Soon she learned her new daddy had all the best treats, and they became true buddies.

Her favorite place to sleep was in our bed. After a couple of restless nights due to her taking up half the bed and chasing rabbits in her dreams, we decided she needed to sleep in the spare bedroom. She had a whole bed to herself, except for nights a kid or one of our other animals would sleep with her. Being an older dog, she was very mellow and had excellent manners. She knew her size, and if she felt like she couldn't squeeze through a space, she would look at me with an expression that said, "Mama you know I can't fit through there!" She did not like for her nails to be touched, and they grew very long. We learned quickly to keep our bare feet away from her. I loved the way she looked and felt. To me, a Mastiff is unlike any other dog. They are very substantial and love to be touched. I loved her smell; it reminded me of warm hay in the summer. When she was diagnosed with hip dysplasia in her golden years, I would give her full body massages to ease her pain. She had a varied diet, loved fruit and for me to cook her fish, squash and beef. She was not a loner and was always by me or her daddy and she had to be touching us. With her paw, muzzle or tail, she had to always have contact with us. And of course "the lean," you know you are loved when a Mastiff leans against you!

During her years we also fostered two other Mastiffs. Both had been kept outside on chains, what a shame. Mastiffs require couches and air conditioning. They will bark when necessary and some will even talk to you. I think they sound like Chewbacca, the wookie from Star Wars. Most importantly, they will give you complete loyalty and love.

We had our Smoochy for five-and-a-half years. As she grew older, her beautiful black mask turned to a lovely gray. She slowed down, her walks became shorter, and many times had to be coaxed to eat. Her world was shrinking and our hearts were breaking as we knew her time was near. For her comfort and ease, we scheduled our vet to come to the house. It happened so quickly but she was surrounded by all those who loved her. Maybe someday we will get another Mastiff and possibly foster again. As for now, we are grieving the loss of our sweet baby.
Melinda Kemppainen - Lawrence, KS

49. Major

Our boy, Major, passed away Easter Sunday and it was a sad day indeed. He was my friend, a stud dog for North Texas Mastiffs, and a special member of our family. At 240 pounds, he would stop traffic wherever he went. He was a perfect ambassador to the breed, in every sense of the word.

As a TDI and TDInc-certified therapy dog, he participated in "Reading to Rover" at local schools and libraries. Children enjoyed lying on his massive, warm coat while they read stories to him. They giggled when he would fall asleep and start snoring.

He also loved to pull my seven grandchildren in wagons and carts.

I learned many valuable lessons from Major, such as being patient and nonjudgmental of others. Never a stranger did he meet, and loved everyone he came in contact with.

He was a very special boy that has left a big void in my heart.
Terri Latva - Gunter, TX

50. Cromwell

This story was posted in a UK newspaper and donated by his owners

A burglar makes the mistake of choosing to rob a 22 stone Mastiff's home. Of all the gardens in the world, the thief had the bad luck of choosing the one where Cromwell was peacefully gnawing on his bone. The three-year-old English Mastiff is a gentle pet, but his breed is also born guard dogs.

Only the thief and Cromwell know what happened next, but it could not have been friendly. The dog's owner, George Watson, 43, was in the shower when he heard a scream and commotion from the back garden. He rushed outside in a towel to find the thief speeding away in a van. Apart from a very agitated dog, the only evidence the man left behind was a torn t-shirt. Mr. Watson assumes Cromwell tore the shirt from the man's back while trying to stop him from stealing their lawnmower which had been taken from the shed and left lying by the gate. At just under 22 stone, the dog could be the world's heaviest, so the man is lucky that his shirt was the only thing shredded.
John and Natasha Jenkins - Norfolk, England

51. Custard

Custard is a special needs dog. As a young puppy he suffered a fit and was rushed to the Royal Canine College of Veterinary Surgeons. They

carried out numerous neurological tests and could not find a cause or repair his damaged brain. Due to his sensitive issue, the breeder decided to keep him.

Unfortunately the other dogs would bully him, and he had to be placed alone in a brick barn with a grass run.

Knowing we owned Cleo, a sweet Mastiff we had from this breeder, she called and asked if we could take Custard. She new Cleo's nature and that she would not bully Custard. Most importantly, she wanted Custard to be living indoors with a family to love him. How could we say no?

After his three-hour car journey, this large two-year-old boy bowled right into our house and plunked himself down in the hallway as if he'd always been there. Cleo adored him as did our two terriers, Maggie and Diesel.

Our vet told us that due to his bad coordination and huge body size, he could afford to lose about two to three stones. Now weighing in at thirteen stones, he still struggles getting up and down.

He loves going to the field for a jog, but must be watched, as he sometimes trips over his own feet and falls.

One beautiful day, a friend and I took him and Cleo to a nearby country park. Custard decided to have a drink from the pool and woops -- he went in head over heels and rolled down the bank into the water. Frantically we rushed into the pool to turn him over, and Cleo jumped in to help us. After we got him on his feet, we then had to haul him up the bank. It was not funny at the time, but hilarious now when I think back on it.

Custard will soon be six years old, and even though he is quite hard work, we would not trade him for the world. When his fluffy wrinkles fall over his eyes, it makes everyone melt. He is my special boy, my "Creamy Custard Cake," and we love him as we love all our dogs.
Sue Epps - Queenborough, Kent, England

52. Tonka

I have the honor to know what it's like to love and be loved by a Mastiff. Throughout my life I have owned many Mastiffs, along with other breeds. I loved them all, but only one stole my heart, Tonka. We had a love that none other could match.

When Tonka came into my life I was living all alone, and she became my world. We were so in tune with each other, just like a finely tuned instrument. I could read her thoughts as well as she could mine. I think she knew me better than I knew myself.

I started putting her in the show ring and she would give it her all. What a sight she was gliding across the ring, head held high and tail wagging. The more she would win, the more shows I would sign up for. During this time I was very sick and had to stop in many states to get my blood transfusions. When I finished, she would always look at me with her sparkling eyes as if to say, "Just keep going; get me there and I will win it."

Tonka won Number One Bitch that year, 1998. She received a collar award and her name printed on the MCOA trophy.

In 1999, the World show was coming up and I had to decide if I should take her out of Specialty and attempt the World Show. Tonka looked at me and said, "Take me Mom, and I will win it."

The show was held at the World Trade Center. Tonka not only won every day, garnishing the titles of International, Mexican, American -- and on the last day -- she won the World Championship. Tonka was the second Mastiff representing the United States to win this and the first bitch to ever do it. This was the most exciting week of our life.

Next she was invited to attend the prestigious Westminster Kennel Club Show, held at Madison Square Garden. She had two body guards surrounding her at all times. She continued to make it up through the ranks and eventually won B.O.B. (Best of Breed). I was so thrilled because this was the first time in 18 years that a bitch had won this title, and my Tonka did it!

In 1999, she won Number Two Mastiff Bitch for the United States.

I retired her that year, bred her for the first time, and she gave me three beautiful puppies.

I lost my sweet Tonka at four-and-a-half years old to Lyme's disease. It was a sad and drawn-out process as her kidneys failed, and there was nothing the vet nor I could do. After spending two weeks at the vet's office, I brought her home. We spent every moment together for the next three days. I held her in my arms as she passed, and God I did not want to let her go. She had been my right-hand girl, my whole life and a part of me left with her that night.

It was very hard for me to adjust to life without her. After spending four-and-a-half wonderful years together, it was hard to go on alone again.

I continued to go to the shows while shedding my tears for her. I miss her so much and the comfort she brought me. My heart will ache until I see her again.

I had Tonka cremated and she is in a marble urn on my desk, right beside me. The following is a tribute to my sweet Tonka:

To See Your Face Again

When your sweet soul and my heart collided, I found the true love nothing else provided.

You put me on top of the world and others felt this way too, when you were named Number One Mastiff of the World, as you will always be so in my heart.

To smell your sweet breath, snuggle my nose close to you.

The cold winter nights with your warmth right beside me.

Yes, what I would not do to see your face again.

There is no stairway to heaven; for if there were, you would be beside me now.

In each rainbow a vision of you comes to me.

I want to thank that sweet soul of yours for our special time together here on earth.

There better be a Rainbow Bridge, for I will make my way there, throw my arms around you and never let go.

Now you be healthy and I will try to be happy because,

The longer you are gone, the longer you are gone, until at last I see your face again.
Sherry Eisenhuth - Tampa, FL

53. Brad Pitt

This is the story of Brad Pitt, the fawn male you see in the picture between the lovely daughters of my Swedish friends who live near my house in Brazil.

I've been involved with dogs ever since I was a child. I first bred "Fila Brasileiros" before breeding Mastiffs which started in August 2000. I began with a fawn bitch named Ully and a brindle male named English Kings Holiday, alias Ney. Both were four years old when they came to my kennel. I tried to mate them many times but Ully was unable to have litters.

Ully lived in our hearts for two years... and died from cancer at the age of six. We all cried for days, but no one felt this loss like Ney. He cried and gave up eating for almost two weeks and I thought he was going to die too. I tried everything to bring him back to life, I even got two more girls to live with him -- the puppies Princess Yasmin and Ingrid.

Thank God those girls brought life back to the house, and Ney was renewed. They were too young to breed with him and I had decided to keep the blood of that boy in my kennel, so I started my search with the old breeder. I discovered that he had mated before, so now I was on a mission to find his puppies, wherever they might be. I finally found a woman with one of his boys, an adult fawn Mastiff, strong and good-looking like his father. This breeder was moving and looking for new homes for her Mastiffs.

Amazingly, she was with litter of this fawn boy and his own daughter. Wow, I was looking for my boy's blood and found puppies from this inbreeding -- who could ask for more? I went to the breeder's home, an abandoned ranch three hours away. She had Artemis (an adult son from my male), a neutered female and their daughter, Petunia, with a litter of two boys and two girls from Artemis, her own father.

I went to her ranch with a breeder I thought I could trust, but time showed me I was wrong (a story I don't want to remember). We saw the puppies, and then I took the breeder to his house. We decided that I would call the lady when I got home to tell her we would take all the dogs (two puppies for me and all the others for him). When I arrived home, I called the breeder and found out that my companion had already returned and picked up all the Mastiffs.

That night he called me saying he did that because he heard she was selling them to someone else, and I could pick up my puppies in a few days. A week later he called asking if he could sell the female pups and I said okay because I only wanted the male. Next he called to tell me my puppy was bitten by a snake and died, now only his pup remained.

A month later he called to say his puppy had been snake-bitten. I drove to his house and took the puppy to the vet. I saw from the markings that this was my puppy. It was a three-month fight, as he was bitten by a Cascavel, the most feared snake in Brazil. We assume he was trying to play with the snake and was bitten in the mouth. The necrosis took away five of his teeth; his liver and kidneys never worked the same again. But even after all this, that fawn boy was marvelous, just like his grandfather, and we decided to call him Brad Pitt (finally his story)...

He was free to come home, but I still had a problem. Ney would never accept another male in the house and would probably kill his own grandson. I found a temporary home nearby with my friend, Christer. It was a big house with two little girls, that showered him with love, and a fawn Mastiff named Monalisa, that was love at first sight.

Brad had a size that could be very intimidating, but no other creature could be more gentle than he. Once, one of the girls brought home a little chicken they named Titi. It was very sickly and assumed to die within a few days. Brad showed the size of his heart by feeding it his own food and keeping it warm. They became best friends for all the years the chicken lived.

A few years later, my old boy Ney died at the age of nine, and I decided it was time to bring Brad home.

I went to Christer's house and, as we were discussing, Brad stood nearby with both girls huddled near him. They knew something was up and they were very uncomfortable.

When we tried to put the leash on Brad, the drama began. I will never forget that moment, as I was cursed by two little girls in Swedish, Portuguese and English, all at the same time. No matter what their parents tried to say or do, the girls and Brad were like one, all together, holding each other like a rock. It was too hard to pull them apart. I could never be responsible for that. I could never sleep in peace again knowing that two children could hate me so much for taking their friend away. I don't care what people may say, but I ensure you that I'm crying now while I write this... just remembering the moment.

I left Brad with Sara and Sophia that day where he lived happily for five-and-a-half years. Sadly I had to put him to sleep, as his liver and kidneys had no more strength to fight. The images of that lovely giant will remain in my mind forever, and also in the hearts of the Bergman family.
Robson Trujillo Marconi - Brazil

54. Sheeba, Bronson & Saber
Gone But Not Forgotten

Sheeba, Bronson and Saber

A million times I've needed you, a million times I've cried. If love alone could have saved you, never would you have died.

In life I loved you dearly; in death I love you still. In my heart you hold a place that no one will ever fill.

If tears could build a stairway and heartache make a lane, I would walk that path to heaven and bring you home again.

Our family chain is broken and nothing feels the same. As God calls us one by one, the chain will link again.

Deeply missed by Mom and Dad.
Laura and Gary Anderson - Beloit, OH

55. Mugsy

My husband and I are dog rescue volunteers. One day we were asked to foster a blind Mastiff. I was apprehensive because I've never cared for a blind dog and was unsure if I could give him the proper care. After my husband and I discussed it, we agreed to take him. How could we say no?

He was the sweetest boy from the very first moment we met him. We taught him to respond to the word "step" whenever there was a change in surface or a step up or down. We were so amazed at how quickly he learned and we, just as quickly, fell in love with him. Soon after, we adopted him and named him Mugsy.

Our trainer recommended that we put him in an obedience class just for socialization. I was hesitant at first, but I took her advice and enrolled him. In the beginning it was hard, because he was overwhelmed by all the other dogs. He had to put all of his trust in me, and thus created our forever bond.

A therapy group was starting and I thought Mugsy would be perfect for it. We trained him for his testing, and I am so proud to say that he earned his CGC and Therapy Dog International titles. With these titles, began a wonderful and amazing journey.

His therapy group visited local nursing homes where I saw miracles happen daily. Residents who had lost their reason to smile began to smile again when they saw Mugsy. We also went to schools to teach children about the importance of pet adoption. Wherever I went, he went. He was my shadow, my heart.

Sadly we lost our sweet Mugsy after two-and-a-half years to Spondylosis. I miss him every minute of every day.

I am forever grateful that he came into our lives; he taught me so much about life. Although he could not see with his eyes, he saw and loved with his heart. He touched everyone that met him and it was a true honor to know him. We continue to rescue, as all dogs are special in their own way. But Mugsy will always hold a dear place in my heart.
Terri Runt - Freeport, IL

56. Fannie

I live on a 20-acre wooded lot where I pursue my passion of raising English Mastiffs. On January 13, 2004, my beautiful 9-month-old, fawn female Mastiff went missing. We discovered a downed tree had damaged the fence where we assume she escaped. It was a very cold 2-degree day with the high expected to be 10. How could my baby survive? Weeks later we had winter weather warnings not to have any skin exposed outside for more than a few minutes, as there was a severe risk of frost bite. My poor baby was somewhere out there in this freezing weather.

We immediately put posters at every intersection for a 20-mile radius. We placed a flier with her picture, reward and description in 700 mailboxes. I contacted shelters, school bus drivers, Fed Ex drivers, meter readers, DNR, Highway Department, Schwann Foods drivers, gas companies for the LP delivery men, vet clinics, postmen, UPS, trash pickup services, radio stations, and Pet Finders. Search and rescue organizations could not help because their dogs are trained to ignore animal scents.

Next we purchased a continuous loop tape and recorded my voice calling her. It was placed outside and played all night. I walked my dogs every day, hoping she was nearby and would hone in on mine or their scent. Every night we awoke at 3 AM, and with a search light, we checked for tracks in the snow.

Mastiffs are not a common breed, and due to their massive size, they draw a lot of attention. I started to worry that someone had her.

One week after she went missing, the temperature dropped to 19 degrees below 0, with wind chills of 45 below. These temperatures lasted about 10 days, and when they let up, we were dumped on with 16 inches of snow in a 5-day period. I could not imagine my very spoiled housedog, just a puppy, being able to survive. This only drove us harder, for we would not stop until she was found, dead or alive.

After 7 long, exhausting weeks, a man showed up at my door and said he saw Fanny. I had been on so many wild goose chases that I was reluctant to get my hopes up. He said he had spotted her while hunting in a wooded, hilly area. We took his 4-wheel-drive back to the woods on some old logging trails and stopped where he said he spotted her. He said she took off like a bullet when she saw him.

I immediately found tracks and knew it was my girl, for no dog around here has the paw size of a Mastiff. We saw many dug-up deer bones, and I started following the tracks and calling her name. I was afraid my voice might make her run after being lost for so long. Eventually, we lost the prints on a very icy part of the trail. Knowing in my heart that it was her paw print, I could not stop, I had to carry on.

After a short while, I sensed something. I looked up a hill to my left -- and to my total disbelief -- there she sat by an old deer stand built on the ground. I immediately started calling her name and heading toward her with this hunter right behind me. She stood up, and I could tell she was about to bolt, so I asked the hunter to stay back. He stopped, and as I continued toward her, she sat back down. As I moved closer, she raised her hackles and started growling at me, baring all her teeth. I crouched but continued toward her, talking in a very soothing voice, and she jumped in the deer stand. I approached it, and she was cowering down but still growling. I knelt down, took off my glove and put my hand near her face. The moment she smelled my hand her tail started wagging. I leapt toward her, wrapped my arms around her neck and sobbed while she licked my tears and every inch of my face. She was reluctant to leave her shelter but soon was comfortable to go with us.

She returned home to a joyous reunion with Pistol and Kiki, my other Mastiffs. I so wanted to prepare her a feast; but since she was so emaciated, I could only give her small portions, which she inhaled.

Within a week she already looked better, no more protruding ribs or hip bones. The most amazing thing was her attitude. She settled right back in as though she had never been away. After 48 days in the cold and wilderness of Wisconsin at only 9-and-a-half months old, I fully expected to have a different dog. But Fanny was amazing, and I still marvel at her strength. I just couldn't stand to look at her without wanting to hug her. She received a closet full of treats, as all her human friends wanted to dote on her. She was very spoiled as she well-deserved.

The pictures are of the day she was found and then two months after.

Our dear sweet Fanny passed away in November 2012.
Tamara Berry - Montello, WI

57. Nala

I have always been an animal lover and worked for many years as a vet tech. I had seen many dogs, but never any the size of an English Mastiff. I remember the first time I saw him, thinking, "What is that?" He was a rich-apricot brindle male who weighed well over 200 pounds, with such a docile temperament. He was definitely one of my favorite patients. One day my husband came into the office to meet me for lunch and saw this "large beast" whom I had talked about quite often. Being the large man that he is, and liking large dogs, he immediately fell in love with him (as did everyone).

For over five years, he kept saying he wanted a Mastiff. Although I loved the breed, I wasn't sure that I was ready for the slobber, smell, etc. Besides, I liked a dog that could keep up with the horses and quads when working on the ranch. I had an old border collie whose time was getting near. I promised my husband that we would replace her with a Mastiff. The day came and we drove several hundred miles to purchase our new family member.

Although this was supposed to be a replacement for "my" border collie, she chose my husband as "hers." I took "Our Spoiled Queen Nala"

everywhere with me; but when my husband was home, she was glued to him. She would sleep soundly until she heard his truck. She could hear him long before I even knew he was home. She would jump to her feet and race to the door wiggling her whole body with excitement. Then the day came when we had to put her down. I have put many animals down, but losing her was one of the hardest things we've ever had to do. My husband was devastated and cried for days. We miss her dearly and I will never forget the Mastiff that changed my life.
Yvonne Jensen - Oroville, CA

58. Little Man

After years of looking for a good breeder and driving hundreds of miles, we finally found our next family member; and a few years later, we had a litter of our own. A litter of fifteen! One of which was a gorgeous reverse brindle male runt. My six-year-old daughter carried him around everywhere and bottle-fed him to supplement since he was getting pushed aside. My brother said he wanted the little guy, and my daughter was very happy she would be able to see him quite often. The day came when he was weaned and ready to go. Unfortunately my brother's landlord said he was going to be too big of a dog, and he could not have him. I had several people who were interested in him due to his color, but when my daughter found out he was going to be sold and not going to her uncle, she could not stop crying.

Being the softy dad that I am, I decided to let her keep him, and what a great decision that has been. They have been completely inseparable. He is constantly by her side and would give his life for her. At only eight months old, my daughter was attacked by the neighbors rottweiler while walking her dog. Most eight-month-old pups would run with fear, but not him. As soon as my daughter screamed, he went into "protective mode," snapping at the rottweiler and chasing him down the driveway.

By the time he was two years old, my daughter had an idea to cart-train him. I inquired about dog carts; but of course he was too large for a dog cart, so I had to buy a miniature horse cart. I didn't think she could train him to pull it, but to my surprise, she not only trained him to pull it, but taught him voice commands as well. She rides in the cart using reins like a horse and words to move him. The two of them have won trophies in parades, have won a 4H Medal of Honor for best out of the whole county, been in a play/performance, and have been asked to be in a commercial. She shares a bunkbed with him and the bottom bunk is completely his. He patiently sits there while she dresses him up in every costume you can think of. He is the most patient, spoiled, BEST dog ever!

Dean Jensen - Oroville, CA

59. BBB

We pulled a two-year-old male Mastiff from the pound (after being there for nine months) the day he was scheduled to be put down (we were notified about him the night beforehand). No other rescues would even go meet him because he had lunged at the dog warden (which obviously was not as bad as it sounds seeing as the warden allowed him nine months in the shelter -- so was my first thought). I went to high school with a fellow rescue worker and we pulled Baby (was his shelter name).

Of course I quickly changed his name to Buddy, where he stayed with us for socializing and adjusting outside the kenneled life he had at the shelter. I found a loving home that was actually a pastor's, and they changed his name to Ben. So we refer to him now as the BBB. He now spends his days working as God's right-hand man in ministries and daily work at the church. Ben was highly misjudged, as we also watched him five months after his adoption, and he was a completely different and healthy happy-looking boy.

Christina Jones - Reynoldsburg, OH

60. Riley

My boy Riley is now two years old and weights 210 pounds.

Riley means the world to me; I have never ever experienced anything like it, the love I feel for my Mastiff is something out of this world.

There isn't a day that goes by without me and my Mastiff spending quality time together. I rush home from work just to be with him. The greetings I receive at the door when I get home melt my heart every single time. I get sooo happy when I see my Mastiff. To be honest with you, my boy has made me a better person. Before bringing my baby home at eight weeks old, I was kind-of missing something in my life. I didn't know what; however, when I got Riley, I knew right away what it was -- it was Riley.

My life completely changed -- my social life -- well there was no social life after Riley. I stopped hanging out after work and throwing my money away in happy hour with coworkers. When he came into my life, I became involved with my community pet owners, and my social life changed for the better Riley became my world, my everything. I started planning my life with Riley in it; I mean everything, no more traveling by planes, we were taking road trips, and we LOVE, LOVE our getaways. I think I know every pet-friendly hotel in the nation, ha!

My point here is, Mastiffs are the BEST companions any human being can ask for; the loyalty, the bond you create with a Mastiff feels human to me. I remember the first time we bonded, that was when I picked him up from the breeder. I got him, we got in the car and drove away. He looked a little confused but, out of nowhere, he just stared at my face for at least five to eight seconds without making a sound, just looking very deep into my eyes. Then he just licked my face and got into my arms and just rested, looking at me from time to time. Right there I knew was the moment when we bonded. I felt that we connected; he accepted me and of course I accepted him as well.

Since then we are glued to each other's hips like crazy. When I'm home is all about Riley. I can't wait for the weekends to do things with my baby. My Mastiff is involved in everything I do; I don't go anywhere without him.

Our favorite thing to do together is swimming, we have been going to a pet-friendly bay for two years now. I love the trust he has in me when we swim together. I love the way we bond when swimming; the connection is amazing, how happy he gets when we swim, I can definitely tell he is enjoying our swim.

His favorite food is cheese; sometimes he won't touch his food unless I put some cheese on it.

He has slept with me and my partner since day one. He was eight weeks old and we couldn't resist this adorable English Mastiff puppy, and brought him to bed, and that was the end of that. Thank God we have a kingsize bed. I get to kiss him goodnight and goodmorning as well! This is one man that truly adores his Mastiff.
Jay Cruz - Hauppauge, NY

61. Winston

Part I

Winston is a service dog, but he wasn't obtained through an expensive organization. Instead, he was picked out from a reputable breeder of health-tested dogs and trained at home as an owner-trained service dog for my father, who is a very large man and needed a very large dog as an assistance animal.

Winston's training began on our very first day together when he was just nine weeks old. For more than a year, he stayed by my side. Every occasion became a fun opportunity to learn, and he loved every minute of it. At four months of age, he passed his first CGC test and Public Access Exam. Thereafter, whether I went to the bank, church, grocery store, restaurant, mall, airport, or any number of other public buildings, he tagged along at my side, fine-tuning his learned abilities and social manners.

I remember excitedly meeting an accredited trainer in a non-profit organization dedicated to training therapy and service dogs. She owned a Bull Mastiff and I just knew she'd love my dog and have something encouraging to remark. Instead, when she saw my Mastiff and heard about my plans for him, she scoffed, rolled her eyes, and blatantly said, "Why'd you get a Mastiff? You'll only get four years of work out of it -- if you can train him at all," and walked away. Her words, while bothersome, didn't get me down. Instead, they had the effect of fueling my desire to continue working with Winston to the best of our ability; and despite her negative statement and obvious skepticism about him among the community, Winston soon became a therapy dog himself -- visiting schools, nursing homes, rehabilitation centers, doctor offices and hospitals.

And by a mere nine months of age, most of his service-task training was complete when he was proficiently able to: fetch the newspaper, put trash in the garbage can, take filled trash bags to the road, load a dishwasher, a sink, and a washing machine, put dirty laundry in a hamper, take clean clothes out of the dryer, fetch any fallen or wanted object, open/close blinds, turn on/off light switches, open the fridge, pull out a beverage to deliver, and close fridge, remove a person's clothing (socks, gloves, jacket, shoes, etc.), fetch an emergency phone, fetch emergency medication, stand for bracing when lifting a person, pull a wheelchair, follow left and right directional cues, put items on counters, pay cashiers, and more.

He now works for my handicapped father and has proven to be a monumental help. Winston is a great example of what hard work and positive reinforcement can accomplish. With a lot of time, dedication, and a few pounds of treats... nothing is impossible. Winston, a Mastiff, has shown that these large animals can be more than couch potatoes and gentle spirits. They have a natural drive to please people, and despite their large size, they can make excellent working dogs.

Part II

When my dad first met Winston, I don't think he fully understood at that time how a gangly puppy could possibly one day become a huge assistance in his life. My father wasn't exactly on board with the idea of a service dog to begin with. He's a man who doesn't like change and had found contentment in doing what he could on his own, and having others do for him what he couldn't. But the rest of the family saw the flaw in this. What if we weren't around to help him? What if he fell and couldn't get up? What if he couldn't reach his medication? A phone in an emergency? It was these things that we worried about in our absence, and as a dog trainer with experience in teaching tasks to owner-trained service dogs, I knew he was a perfect candidate for a service animal himself.

Then came Winston; he was all tongue and legs, and as a puppy, he had to learn the same good manners as any other dog: housebreaking, crating, no chewing, no jumping, etc. Needless to say, my father wasn't very impressed with the occasional puddle on the floor or the muddy paws landing on his clean shirt. But as I worked with Winston, and he learned and matured, it wasn't long at all before he became a constant and beloved presence in the household.

When Winston was 10 weeks old, he learned how to open and close doors by tugging on a rope tied to the door handle, and then pawing the door to slam it closed. This was his first official service dog task. And when my dad saw it in an action, you could practically see the flicker of excitement build in his eyes.

At 12 weeks, Winston entered into an International Dog Show, where he won Best of Breed and numerous medals. This wasn't service dog related, but when we came home and displayed his accomplishments, the excitement in dad's eyes began to morph into something akin to pride. My father began to see Winston as something more than a dog -- he was a winner, and a couple weeks later after earning his CGC, he was practically a "prodigy." My dad still didn't think he needed a service dog, but now he was intrigued.

Before Winston was four months old, he learned how to gently remove clothing from a person's body, and pick up and deliver fallen objects to a person. It was during our first trip to the doctor's office with Dad that I think my father truly started imagining how much better life with a service dog could be. We waited in the waiting room for over an hour, and during that time, Winston and I didn't waste a second of it. Among basic obedience we also practiced removing my gloves, delivering medicine bottles to nearby patients, and picking up anything that I would "accidentally" drop during a heel. The other patients, and even some of the staff, watched Winston with awe and smiled; and the mood in this otherwise heavy atmosphere was momentarily lifted during our exercises. My dad watched and listened to others comment on how their lives could change with a dog like Winston, and suddenly my dad started nodding his head and agreed with those total strangers, remarking on how much this dog had accomplished already and what all he was going to be able to do for him in the future.

So while my dad's feelings toward a service dog may have changed, it wasn't until a few weeks later that his feelings for Winston, as the individual, intensified. When Winston was four-months, he became suddenly and violently ill. He dropped a notable amount of weight, became lethargic, and vomited until there was nothing left to expel. It was actually my dad that first noticed these signs and it was Dad who insisted that Winston go to the vet immediately. And thank God he did, because as it turned out, Winston had developed a blockage and needed immediate surgery or he'd have died before morning. The vet found a chunk of corn cob lodged in his intestine (which we still don't know how Winston got), and thought it best to keep Winston at the clinic to keep him on fluids and under observation for a few days. The level of care and concern my dad showed in those days and the ones that followed was tremendous. He needed constant status reports to calm his worry and anxiety. I actually received a phone call from the vet giving me an update and then he jokingly tacked on, "And you can tell your dad to stop calling." The uncertainty of losing Winston made a huge impact on my father. The day that Winston was released from the vet clinic was the day that my dad became the president of Winston's fan club.

Post-blockage, Winston had publicly become Dad's pride and joy, and thereafter he was invested in and encouraging toward his training. He even starting bringing home bags of treats each week just to spoil his baby boy. Seeing the love he had toward Winston, I knew that the hours of training each day with every second, that all the time invested, was going to great use. My dad has been using Winston as a service dog around the house for nearly two years now, and he's still as in love with this Mastiff as the day he came home from the vet after a near-death experience. Was it hard to give Winston up? Absolutely. But the help, companionship and happiness that he brings to my dad is what it's all about. And I'm blessed to still have Winston in the family, and nearby too, so I can visit him often.

Rebecca Deaver - Clanton, AL

EPILOGUE

This book contains a mere sampling of all the amazing stories about English Mastiffs. Some of the best stories were told to me verbally and never submitted for this book. I hope in the future I will have the privilege of sharing those beautiful tales.

The first purpose of this book is to educate those who are not familiar with this majestic breed. Many people are intimidated by their size and may compare them to other Mastiff breeds. As the stories prove, the English is the first and ultimate Mastiff. They are commonly known as gentle giants, and rightly so.

The second purpose of this book is to raise funds for all English Mastiffs in need.

I consider this book a chicken soup for the Mastiff soul. The pictures alone speak volumes; and when you look into their eyes, you can see their warm and gentle soul.

I believe the statement, "A dog is man's best friend," was coined perfectly for the English Mastiff. There is no other breed that can surpass them in loyalty, devotion and love.

All proceeds from this book will go to RFI (Rescue Foundation Inc.) in New York City, USA. With your donation ,we will be able to save many Mastiffs all across the United States of America.

Thank you for purchasing this book and I hope you enjoyed it.

Millie Spillers

We're going to check out the house

I'm in the kitchen and I smell something

Made in the USA
Middletown, DE
18 May 2022